SANTA CRUZ
TRAINS

SIDETRACKED
LAUREL & GLENWOOD

Derek R. Whaley

*Dedicated to Stanley D. Stevens (1933–2022),
who has been an endless source of motivation
and encouragement to me for the past ten years.
You are missed but will never be forgotten.*

First edition, March 2023
First revision, April 2023
Second revision, April 2024

Published by Zayante Publishing
Santa Cruz, California
www.ZayantePublishing.com

ISBN 978-1-953609-16-8

Publisher's Cataloging-in-Publication data
Whaley, Derek R., 1983–
    Sidetracked : Laurel & Glenwood / Derek R. Whaley.—1st ed.
    Santa Cruz Trains
    128 p. : ill. ; 23 cm
    Includes bibliography.
ISBN 978-1-953609-16-8
1. Santa Cruz County (Calif.)—History. 2. Scotts Valley (Calif.)—
History. 3. Glenwood (Calif.)—History. 4. Laurel (Calif.)—
History. 5. South Pacific Coast Railroad Company—History. 6.
Southern Pacific Railroad Company—History. 7. Railroads—
California—Santa Cruz County—History. 8. California—
History, Local. I. Whaley, Derek R. 1983–. II. Title. III. Series.
F868 .S3 W43 2023
979.471

CONTENTS

No. 30. MAIN LINE TRAINS March 28th, 1886.

FROM SAN FRANCISCO. | | | | | | | | | | | NAMES OF STATIONS. | | | | | TOWARD SAN FRANCISCO.

25	23	21	13	11	9	7	5	3	1	STATIONS	2	4	6	8	10	12	14	20	22	24
C	C	B	B	A	B	A	C	B	B		D	B	C	A	B	A	B	C	B	C
			4 30	4 45	2 30	8 30	8 30	8 00	0	Lv. SAN FRANCISCO Ar.	80.6	1.00	8 05	6 35	11 05	9 35				
				4 45	2 45	8 45	9 15		3.0	ALAMEDA MOLE	77.6		7 46	6 16	10 46	9 16				
								5 00	2 00	ALAMEDA POINT		12 00	8 30							
			4 53	2 53	8 53	8 23	5 02	2 02	5 6	ALAMEDA JUNC'N	75.0	11 58	8 28	7 39	16 09	10 40	9 09			
			4 56	2 56	8 56	8 26	5 05	2 05	6 4	PACIFIC AVE.	74.2	11 55	8 25	7 36	16 06	10 37	9 06			
			4 59	2 59	8 59	8 29	5 10		7 2	THIRD AVE	73.4		8 20	7 33	6 03	10 34	9 03			
			5 05	3 05	9 06	8 34	5 30	2 30	9 3	PARK ST	71.3	11 35	8 05	7 26	5 57	10 29	8 57			
			5 08	3 08	9 09	8 37	5 35	2 35	10 2	HIGH ST	70.4	11 31	7 55	7 23	5 51	10 27	8 54			
			5 17	3 18	9 19	8 45	5 55	2 55	14 5	W. SAN LEANDRO	66.1	11 16	7 20	7 13	5 44	10 18	8 45			
			5 23	3 23	9 24	8 50	6 05	3 05	16 8	W. SAN LORENZO	63.8	11 00	7 05	7 08	5 39	10 15	8 40			
			5 27	3 28	9 29	8 54	6 15	3 16	19 0	RUSSELLS.	51.6	10 50	6 50	7 03	5 35	10 12	8 35			
			5 32	3 31	9 33	8 56	6 25	3 22	20 4	MT. EDEN.	60.2	10 45	6 40	7 00	5 32	10 10	8 32			
			5 40	3 39	9 41	9 03	6 45	3 50	24 2	ALVARADO	56.4	10 30	5 50	6 52	5 22	10 03	8 23			
			5 42	3 41	9 43	9 05	6 55	4 10	25 1	HALLS	55.5	10 20	5 32	6 50	5 18	10 01	8 40			
			5 51	3 51	9 53	9 17	6 11	4 47	29 4	NEWARK	51.2	9 65	4 49	6 41	5 08	9 50	8 11			
			5 55	3 55	9 57	9 17	6 21	4 50	31 6	MOWRYS	49 0	9 45	4 39	6 37	5 04	9 45	8 07			
			6 10	4 09	10 11	9 31	8 58	5 38	37 9	ALVISO	42 7	9 30	3 54	6 23	4 49	9 30	7 52			
			6 17	4 14	10 16	9 36	9 24	6 00	40 5	AGNEWS	40 1	8 45	3 28	6 17	4 42	9 24	7 46			
			6 25	4 20	10 23	9 42	9 45	6 25	43 6	SANTA CLARA	37 0	8 15	3 05	6 11	4 35	9 17	7 34			
A. M.		6 30	6 32	4 29	10 30	9 48	10 30	6 50	46 2	SAN JOSE	34 4	7 45	2 05	6 02	4 24	9 09	7 30	6 20		
7 08		7 18	6 45	4 41	10 41	10 00	11 10	50 9	CAMPBELL	29 7		1 35	5 52	4 12	8 57	7 18	5 50		
		7 48	6 55	4 51	10 51	10 10	11 48	55 5	LOS GATOS	25 3		1 00	5 42	4 01	8 46	7 08	5 20		
		8 36		5 00	11 00	10 18	12 30	58 1	ALMA	22.5		12 30	5 31	3 51	8 36		4 50		
		9 06		5 13	11 13	10 31	1 00	62 4	WRIGHTS	18 2		11 55	5 23	3 38	8 24		4 18		
		9 20		5 21	11 20	10 36	1 22	64 4	HIGHLAND	16 2		11 40	5 16	3 30	8 17		3 55		
		9 46		5 27	11 26	10 44	1 45	65 8	GLENWOOD	14 8		11 10	5 10	3 24	8 11		3 35		
19 Pass. B				5 40	11 39	10 57	2 18	70 0	DOUGHERTY'S M'L	10 6	15 Mixed A. M.	10 30	4 58	3 09	7 57	18 Mixed A			
P. M.	A. M.	P. M.		5 52	11 54	11 09	2 47	73 5	FELTON	7 1	16 Mixed B	9 50	4 47	2 56	7 45			
2.15	8 00	2 00	11 00					6 50	80 8	BOULDER CR'K	11 4	10 45				12 40			6 40	5 30
2.18	8 05	2 03	11 05					7 00	80 2	LORENZO	13 8	10 40				12 35			6 35	5 25
2.34	8 20	2 24	11 25					7 20	77 2	PACIFIC MILLS	10 8	10 20				12 15			6 15	5 10
2.50	8 35	2 40	11 45					7 40	73 5	FELTON	7 1	10 00				11 55			5 55	4 50
	8 35	3 00		5 52	11 54	11 09	2 56	73 5	FELTON	7 1		9 50	4 47	2 56	7 45		11 09 11 09	8 52 5 45	
	8 38	3 10		5 54	11 53	11 13	3 04	74 3	BIG TREES	6 3		9 43	4 42	2 52	7 42		10 50	5 40	
	8 48	4 00		6 02	12 01	11 21	3 24	76 8	RINCON	3 8		9 26	4 34	2 44	7 31		10 40	5 30	
	8 57	4 20		6 12	12 10	11 30	3 45	79 6	SANTA CRUZ	1 0		9 08	4 25	2 30	7 25		10 30	5 20	
	9 05	4 30		6 20	12 15	11 35	3 55	80 6	Ar. ST'A CRUZ B'CH Lv.	0		9 00	4 05	2 10	7 10		10 20	5 10	
	A. M.	P. M.		P. M.	P. M.	A. M.	P. M.				A. M.	A. M.	P. M.	P. M.	A. M.		A. M.	P. M.	

*—Trains stop only on Signal or to leave Passengers. †—Trains do not stop for Passengers. A—Daily. B—Sundays Excepted. C—Sundays Only. D—Saturdays Excepted.

FULL FACE FIGURES denote meeting and passing places, and Trains will to all cases stop.
Trains Nos. 7, 8, 11 and 12 will stop on signal at Arffs and Alviso Draw Bridges.
Engine and crew running Trains 13 and 14 will have use of Main Track between Glenwood and New Felton between hours of 9.46 A. M. and 3 35 P. M., avoiding Regular Trains.
Trains Nos. 7 and 12, meet on double track. In case of delay, No. 7 must not pass High St. until 30 minutes behind the opposing train's time. Through trains will be governed by same rules as Locals between Alameda Mole and Alameda Junction.
All Mixed Trains will have Freight Trains rights.
Casey's is not a Flag Station on this card.

Train No. 10 will take Siding for Train No. 7.
Train No. 5 can have until 8.50 A. M. to meet Train No. 12 at San Leandro. No. 12 takes siding.
Trains and Engines C. F. and 8. F. Railroads have preference to track at crossings. Engineers will come to a full stop and sound whistle before crossing.
No two Trains will pass each other at Stations on Double Track through Alameda. All Regular Morning Trains running North will have preference into Stations. Regular Trains in afternoon, going South, will have preference. All Extra Trains will avoid Regular Trains at Stations.
In case of delay, all Main Line Trains will wait at Felton thirty minutes for connecting Trains on F. and P. Branch, and run thirty minutes late, unless otherwise ordered.

A. H. WALKER,
Train Dispatcher.

L. FILLMORE,
General Superintendent.

Employee timetable showing the schedule for the main line of the South Pacific Coast Railroad, March 28, 1886. Note Laurel is called Highland and Edric and Clems do not appear at all. (*Pacific Coast Narrow Gauge*)

INTRODUCTION

Life in the Santa Cruz Mountains on California's Central Coast would have been very different had it not been for the railroad. The main route through the mountains prior to 1880 was via the McKiernan Toll Road and the Santa Cruz Gap Turnpike, which linked Santa Cruz to the Santa Clara Valley. This was an ancient trail originally used by the Awaswas-speaking peoples before the Spanish and Mexican governments transformed it into the Franciscan Trail.

'Mountain Charlie' McKiernan settled beside the Laguna del Sargento on the Summit in 1851 and immediately set about improving the route south from his ranch to the vicinity of modern-day Scotts Valley. When the Santa Cruz Gap Turnpike was completed to the Summit in April 1858, McKiernan and others incorporated the Santa Cruz Turnpike Company, which was tasked with upgrading McKiernan's road into a turnpike. The improved toll road opened on October 16, 1858, making the Bean Creek area widely accessible to the public for the first time. Gradually, this area transitioned from logging to farming and fruit-growing and became the community known as Glenwood.

Meanwhile, a little over one mile to the east as the crow flies, similar activities were bringing another community to life. The northwest corner of the former Rancho Soquel Augmentation had remained unused and mostly inaccessible since it was first granted to Martina Castro in 1844. A few settlers, some legitimate owners and others squatters, moved into the gulches along the northwestern reaches of the property along the West Branch of Soquel Creek. Lyman John Burrell moved into the area in 1853, settling on a large property with his home situated on the ridge and additional lands reaching down to a tributary of Soquel Creek afterwards called Burrell (later Laurel) Creek. John Schultheis also settled on the summit around 1853, later building a road to connect his home near the Summit to the railroad station below. Meanwhile, David Burns moved to the area in the late 1850s, settling alongside the creek later named after him, beside which he operated a small shingle mill. In 1860, Hiram Morrell arrived at the area and, four years later, married Clara, the youngest daughter of Burrell. Morrell operated a small mill near the Summit. These families named their sprawling mountain-top community Highland.

On April 22, 1863, a long-fought lawsuit over the fate of the Augmentation Ranch finally came to an end. Most of the people living in the area were confirmed in possession, and others benefited greatly from the decision. The true victor of the suit, however, was Frederick A. Hihn. Through careful purchases in the late 1850s and early 1860s, Hihn had acquired claims to massive portions of the former rancho, with the settlement awarding him 6,280 acres and purchases made during the lawsuit granting him another 6,889 acres. Among his acquisitions was Tract 16, which encompassed most of the headwaters of the West Branch of Soquel Creek below Highland. At the time, there was no easy way to transport timber harvested from here, so Hihn bided his time and focused on other ventures in Aptos and Santa Cruz.

The establishment of turnpikes across the Summit led to the creation of destination resorts in the Santa Cruz Mountains. While hostelries were not uncommon along any public road, these resorts were designed specifically to entice people to stay, often for a whole month in the summer. The appealing mix of redwood forest, sandy chaparral hilltops, and natural spring waters attracted visitors from across the Bay Area and beyond. Hotel de Redwood near the junction of the Santa Cruz Gap Turnpike and the Soquel Turnpike was established around 1870, with Glenwood Magnetic Springs at the top of Branciforte Creek and DeWolfe's Magnetic Springs on Bean Creek following in the mid-1870s. All three resorts advertised the medicinal benefits of water from nearby springs, with Hotel de Redwood capitalizing on sulfur-rich water and the latter two fixated on iron-rich 'magnetic' water.

Construction of the South Pacific Coast Railroad beginning in December 1877 brought its own blend of unique personalities. Tunnel construction and grading crews were composed primarily of Chinese workers, while bridge and tunnel support crews were generally Cornish or Irish. Fights were common between members of different crews and the work itself was treacherous. Several Chinese workers died in landslides above Burns Creek. Boring of the tunnel to Wrights began in October 1878 but the construction was delayed repeatedly due to weather, worker strikes, and two deadly explosions in the tunnel.

Together, these crews constructed around a dozen bridges and half-bridges above Burns, Burrell, and Bean Creeks and built three tunnels. Tunnel No. 2 was the longest built by the railroad at 6,157 feet. It marked the highest point on the route and also passed under the summit of the Coast Range, so was appropriately nicknamed the Summit Tunnel. This tunnel was renumbered Tunnel No. 1 in 1909 when the route was standard gauged and after a tunnel on Los Gatos Creek was dismantled. Tunnel No. 3 (later No. 2) was the second longest at 5,793 feet and connected the Soquel Creek and Bean Creek basins. It sometimes went by the names Glenwood Tunnel or Laurel Tunnel, depending on the direction of travel. This tunnel passes beneath both Highway 17 and the former Glenwood Highway (Glenwood Drive). The final tunnel, Tunnel No. 4 (later No. 3), was much shorter at only 913 feet and passed beneath the McKiernan Toll Road (Mountain Charlie Road). As a result, it is generally referred to as the Mountain Charlie Tunnel.

The completion of the railroad in May 1880 turned the Santa Cruz Mountains into the playground of the Bay Area elite. Every summer, hundreds of families left their comfortable urban lives to relax in the relatively tamed nature along the railroad's mountain route. Some of their primary destinations were those rustic resorts that had existed before the advent of the railroad. But soon, more mountain hotels appeared, especially around the Glenwood area. Mt. Pleasant Farm, the Glenwood Hotel, Villa Fontenay, and Gibbs' Resort all catered more to adventurous outdoorspeople than those seeking medicinal help. However, the railroad was only somewhat interested in holidaymakers and commuters. Its main focus was freight.

When the South Pacific Coast Railroad was still searching for a way to connect the Santa Clara Valley to Santa Cruz, it found several viable options. It was Hihn, Charles Martin of Glenwood, and a few other men who convinced the railroad's president, Alfred Davis, to take a more meandering route to reach Santa Cruz. By directing the railroad through Hihn's Augmentation lands and the Bean Creek basin, the railroad could ultimately access the vast redwood forests of the San Lorenzo Valley. As a bonus, logging firms between Wrights and Zayante Creek, as well as fruit growers, and other freight concerns along this route, could more easily ship out their products.

Over a period of sixty years, several freight customers operated along the three-mile section of track between the Summit Tunnel and the Mountain Charlie Tunnel. In Highland, Hihn leased his land to interested parties who harvested splitstuff and shipped it out by train. This helped the community grow into its own distinct settlement named Laurel. In 1900, the F. A. Hihn Company erected a large-scale mill below Laurel and processed lumber there intermittently until the start of World War I. A short-lived freight stop, Edric, was set up near the Summit Tunnel to support the transport of logs from the headwaters of Burns Creek to the mill far below. In the Bean Creek area, small-scale logging persisted throughout the region as long as the railroad operated. One of the lumber firms, E. A. Clem & Company, even managed to have a station registered to support its operation. The railyard at Glenwood, meanwhile, served as a vital assembly area for long lumber-laden trains heading to the Bay Area.

This book explores the history of these stations, tunnels, resorts, and commercial ventures in more detail, accompanied by over 100 historical and contemporary photographs and maps. While it is light on technical terminology, some terms cannot be avoided. The name of the railroad company that operated across this section changed over the years. It began as the narrow-gauge South Pacific Coast Railroad. In 1887, it was reincorporated as the South Pacific Coast Railway and promptly leased and later sold to the Southern Pacific Railroad. It continued to operate under its old name until the line was completely standard gauged between 1907 and 1909. The tunnels in this book are described according to railroad geography, which means west is *towards* San Francisco and east is *away from* San Francisco. Thus, tunnel portals may be described as east or west even when geographically-speaking they should be the opposite. All other directions are based on real-world geography. Regarding trackage, a spur is usually a short section of track that breaks off from the mainline and dead-ends. A siding, on the other hand, breaks off but then connects back to the mainline at a later point. The terms 'bridge' and 'trestle' are used interchangeably since all of the railroad bridges along this section used the bent and crossbeam frames of the trestle style.

Photographic material used in this book came from a wide range of sources. Thanks goes to the Bancroft Library, the California State Library, Jim Cirner, Jeff Escott, Edward Fenn, Jack Hanson, History San José, Richard Holland, Ralph Leidy, Bruce MacGregor, Michael Maslan, the Mount Hermon Association, Ginger Constantine Navarrete, Gil Pennington, George Pepper, the Santa Cruz Museum of Art & History, the Santa Cruz Public Library, Michael J. Semas, the Sourisseau Academy, Jay Topping, Ronnie Trubek, UC Davis, UC Santa Cruz, and Jim Vail. Special thanks for research assistance to Jonathan Bates, Henry Bender, the California State Archives, the California State Railroad Museum, Brian Liddicoat, Duncan Nanney, Marla Novo, Lisa Robinson, Joe Shreve, and Stanley Stevens, among others. Additional thanks to Kara Kennedy, Lindsay Breach, Kanda Whaley, and Karen Samsom for editorial assistance on short notice. And as always, thanks to the generosity and support of the members of the Santa Cruz Trains Facebook Group—this book would not exist without your help and contributions.

A dog begging for food through a window in Laurel, while a woman looks on, circa 1890. (*Santa Cruz Museum of Art & History*)

Standard-gauge tracks and two short trestles between Edric and Laurel in the upper Burns Creek area, circa 1910. (*Author's collection*)

EDRIC

Edric was the last station established along the Southern Pacific Railroad's route between the Summit Tunnel and the Mountain Charlie Tunnel. It was also the only one to be abandoned prior to the closure of the railroad line in 1940. However, it was an important landmark long before it ever became a station.

During construction of the Summit Tunnel between 1878 and 1880, work crews lived on the hillsides around the east portal of the tunnel. Stereographs from around 1880 show at least two structures around the tunnel, likely worker cottages abandoned after the railroad was completed. These workers would have also been responsible for building the four trestles and numerous half-bridges above Burrell and Burns Creeks. The most substantial of these structures crossed Burns Creek immediately outside the east portal of Summit Tunnel. Early photographs show a short, open-deck bridge that sat immediately outside the tunnel's portal. Following a punishing winter storm in 1890, the structure was replaced with a sturdier bridge, which was subsequently superseded by a standard-gauge bridge around 1908. Remains of this third structure can still be found in Burns Creek.

The completion of the railroad right-of-way from Felton to the Summit Tunnel in January 1880 made removing debris from the tunnel much easier. Hopper cars were likely brought in so material could be removed directly from the tunnel to places that needed filling. Once the tunnel was completed in April, crews packed up and left. Other than the small-scale logging operations, little happened in the area around Burns Creek for twenty years. An unusual photograph showing at least ten people seeming to wait for a train outside the tunnel portal is the only hint that there was some activity near the Summit Tunnel at this time.

Things began to change at the end of 1899, when the F. A. Hihn Company realized that its lumber mill on Gold Gulch outside Felton had nearly run out of viable timber. Early the next year, the company began the arduous task of re-locating the mill's machinery to the confluence of Burns and Laurel Creeks with the intention of opening a new mill the following year. By November 1900, lumber production at the mill was in full swing. For at least the first two years, most of the timber was hauled down to the mill from the headwaters of Burns Creek north of the Summit Tunnel. Getting this timber to the mill was a diffi-cult task that involved a cable incline capable of lowering flatcars down to the mill from the railyard at Laurel. However, transporting the cut timber to Laurel required something else: it needed a railroad station.

At some point in 1901, the Southern Pacific Railroad added a new station to its roster: Edric. Deriving its name from Frederick Hihn, the station was likely established as the junction between the railroad line and a spur track that ran a short distance up Burns Creek to collect logs for the mill. A 134-foot-long spur was recorded at the site, though this was likely a separate spur that ran alongside the mainline for a short distance. The mill probably only used its spur for a few years, but Southern Pacific found another use for the station.

For nearly a decade, Southern Pacific had been working to upgrade the route of the South Pacific Coast Railway to standard gauge. By the time of the April 1906 earthquake, standard-gauge track had been extended as far as Wrights. The next major task was to enlarge the tunnels and standard gauge the tracks between Wrights and Santa Cruz. The spur at Edric was a useful place to park material and railroad cars used in this construction work. Also, because of the remoteness of the area, workers may have lived on site, so space was required for them as well. In late 1905, Edric was added to employee timetables as a freight stop, and its spur may have been lengthened to 234 feet in late 1908, although this may have been a clerical error.

Unfortunately for Edric, the station could not withstand Mother Nature. In January 1909, a destructive winter storm struck the Santa Cruz Mountains causing major damage to the not-yet-reopened line. At Edric, a massive land-slide moved 200 feet of track 15 feet downhill towards Burns Creek. Thirty-four cars fell into the creek and the spur they had been parked on was a complete loss. The tunnel had reopened the previous year, meaning the usefulness of the station had come to an end. When the right-of-way was repaired and the line reopened a few months later, the spur was not rebuilt. In October, Edric was removed from timetables. The only evidence of the station that remained was a short spur on the west bank of the Burns Creek bridge where the tunnel repair car was stored.

A South Pacific Coast Railroad train emerging from the east portal of the Summit Tunnel. Piles of firewood, worker cabins, and debris suggests this image dates to slightly after the tunnel was completed, circa 1880.(*Author's collection*)

A stereograph of the same scene as the previous page with a man holding a lamp standing on the tracks in the foreground, circa 1880. (*Gil Pennington*)

A South Pacific Coast Railway pile driver car pushed by locomotive no. 13 somewhere along the trackage above Burns Creek. This may have been repair work done in response to storm damage in 1890. (*UC Santa Cruz*)

The railroad east portal of the Summit Tunnel, now with a shed and platform. Passengers wait for the train to emerge. The trestle over Burns Creek appears new, suggesting this photo was taken after the bridge was replaced following the 1890 storms. (*Santa Cruz Museum of Art & History*)

The east portal of the Summit Tunnel following its upgrade to support standard-gauge trains, circa 1920s. (*Author's collection*)

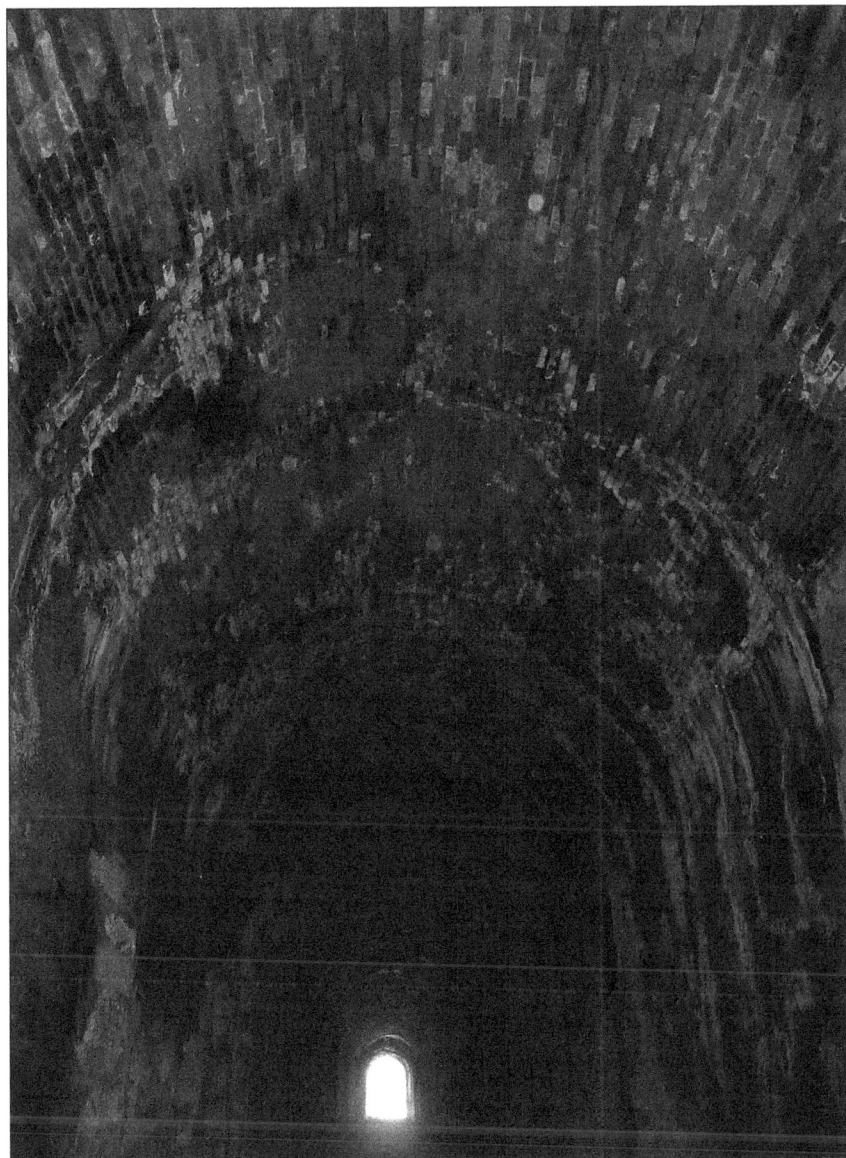

View inside the Summit Tunnel looking toward the east portal, 2013. Note the brick ceiling supporting the unstable sandstone above it. Nearly 300 feet of this tunnel remains intact. Photo by Derek R. Whaley. (*Author's collection*)

Southern Pacific Railroad survey photographs documenting storm damage at Edric above Burns Creek, late January 1909. A 200-foot-long landslide here shifted the track 15 feet downhill, throwing 34 cars into Burns Creek far below. (*Above and opposite: Neil Vodden Collection, courtesy Jack Hanson*)

A passenger train crossing a half-trestle above Burns Creek heading toward the Summit Tunnel, circa 1920. (*Santa Cruz Museum of Art & History*)

A double-headed *Sun Tan Special* train crossing a trestle on approach to Laurel, July 9, 1939. Photo by Wilbur C. Whittaker. (*Jim Vail*)

Southern Pacific locomotive no. 2381 pulling a commuter train around the final curve into Laurel, July 9, 1939. Photo by Wilbur C. Whittaker. (*Jim Vail*)

Post-1940 storm survey photo of the right-of-way east of Laurel, with two hoppers parked on an overgrown siding, April 4, 1940. (*Bruce MacGregor*)

#11 MP L-62.6 east end Tunnel #1 facing west at slide st east end trestle 62.64 2-29-40

Post-1940 storm survey photo of the right-of-way outside the east portal of the Summit Tunnel, February 29, 1940. A tunnel repair car sits on a spur beside the Burns Creek bridge. (*Bruce MacGregor*)

The remains of the Burns Creek bridge, taken outside the east portal of the Summit Tunnel, April 1954. Photo by Paul L. Henchey. (*UC Davis*)

SIDETRACKED

Modern views of the east portal of the Summit Tunnel, July 20, 2014. The concrete portal is still intact with its date visible overhead. Remains of the Burns Creek bridge also still stand. Photos by Derek R. Whaley. (*Author's collection*)

Plat of Laurel, showing building locations and the South Pacific Coast Railway right-of-way, circa 1900. (*UC Santa Cruz*)

LAUREL

The Summit Tunnel was only one of several tunnels built by the South Pacific Coast Railroad in the late 1870s to link the Bay Area with Santa Cruz. Just over half a mile away to the west, another tunnel was needed to connect the Soquel Creek basin with the Bean Creek valley. When railroad crews first moved into the area, they encountered only virgin redwood forest. Two opportunistic lumbermen, Harold F. Elbone and John Peter Houck, leased land from Frederick Hihn and built a small lumber mill near the railroad grade. From this, they provided ties, posts, bents, beams, and firewood for the railroad's construction crews.

Construction of the tunnel to Glenwood began in May 1879, with Chinese crews working from both ends. Frederick Hihn provided the right-of-way and permission to cut through his Soquel Creek properties, while Charles Martin in Glenwood did the same for the other end of the tunnel. The firm of Martin, Ballard & Ferguson was responsible for its construction and the firm's crews encountered few issues with the project. The material encountered by the boring team was almost solid granite, which required large explosives to blast through but resulted in few cave-ins. In fact, much of the interior of the tunnel did not require timberwork because the interior walls were so solid. In June, a record was set with 509 feet of tunnel drilled in one day. Crews completed the tunnel in December and then moved on to build bridges above Burrell and Burns

Creeks and assist in the Summit Tunnel's construction.

For a brief period, the mill, the railroad workers, and their support crews gave life to the area, which became associated with Highland, the settlement at the top of the ridge. To underline this connection, John Schultheis built a short road between the Santa Cruz Gap Turnpike and the railroad grade in 1880 to make it easier for local ranchers and farmers to ship their goods. This road is likely what prompted the South Pacific Coast Railroad to establish a depot there before the route opened in May 1880. With the completion of the railroad, though, most of the temporary residents left and activity around the station declined. Elbone and Houck continued to operate their mill for a number of years to provide fuel wood to passing trains, but Glenwood, just a mile to the west, also provided this service, leading the mill to eventually close. Another lumber venture by Ephraim Morrell beginning in 1881 attempted to produce commercial-grade lumber along Cleveland Gulch, just to the south of the station. But Morrell gave up in 1885. Not long after, Joshua Barber leased the land and attempted to drill for oil, but with no luck.

Few people lived year-round in the vicinity of the station; however, seasonal traffic was steady, especially once the road to Hotel de Redwood was completed in late 1885. This made Highland the destination for travelers hoping to vacation at the well-known resort. The surrounding community adopted the name Laurel in 1882 when residents established a school near the station. The settlement's name is derived from a local species of tree, the California bay laurel (*Umbellularia californica*). In November of that year, a post office under the same name was established, probably in a small general store that was built across Schulties Road from the station. Gradually, even Burrell Creek was renamed Laurel Creek. The last holdout was the South Pacific Coast Railroad, which refused to change the station's name until mid-1887, when it was taken over by the Southern Pacific Railroad.

Laurel was never a thriving settlement. Besides the school, the village was composed primarily of a general store and a small hotel. For the period from 1880 to 1900, the settlement existed solely to cater to Hotel de Redwood customers and to service the freight needs of Summit residents who lived closer to Laurel than Wrights. The South Pacific Coast Railroad never even bothered to build a depot at the site—that responsibility fell to the Southern Pacific Railroad in 1887. The depot provided year-round passenger and freight agency services, and also hosted a Wells Fargo Express office.

Frederick Hihn had been a champion of the small community throughout this time, which makes sense since he owned most of the land in the basin. But he also knew that he would need to access the area at some point in the future. That moment came in February 1900, when his F. A. Hihn Company began moving machinery from its Gold Gulch lumber mill in Felton to the confluence of Laurel and Burns Creeks. The influx of lumbermen, many of whom would work year-round at this mill, revitalized Laurel. From 1900 to early 1906, over 100 men, many bringing along their families, shifted their lives to the mountain hamlet. They erected homes and cottages along the hillsides and built up the tiny business district beside the railroad tracks by adding a livery stable and blacksmith shop. The schoolhouse quadrupled its purpose, acting sometimes as a dance hall, a church, or a town hall. Tourists came to observe the mill's operations and explore nature. Then the earthquake struck and the short heyday came to a sudden end.

The 1906 earthquake ruined everything for Laurel. The village itself survived relatively unharmed, but both tunnels were blocked by debris. Railroad crews were able to reopen the tunnel to Glenwood relatively quickly, but only local narrow-gauge traffic could pass that way. For over a year, tourism and freight were put on hold. The Hihn Company relocated most of its machinery to Kings Creek north of Boulder Creek, briefly abandoning its Laurel mill until the railroad route to the Bay Area was restored.

In September 1907, the Summit Tunnel was reopened and the tunnel to Glenwood was promptly shut down so it could be upgraded to standard gauge. Suddenly Laurel found itself the eastern terminus of the Southern Pacific Railroad's route through (or rather to) the mountains. The Hihn Company used this opportunity to resume limited milling in spring 1908, but the mill shut down after only a month due to poor demand. Passenger service to Laurel from the Bay Area also resumed at this time, but the Panic of 1907 had made people cautious in their spending, resulting in lackluster summer traffic.

Laurel never really recovered from the earthquake. The mill eventually reopened, but its output was reduced until it finally shut its doors at the end of 1913. The settlement was not located along a major thoroughfare   Glenwood Highway ran to the west and the San José-Santa Cruz Road ran to the east—and interest in remote mountain destinations along railroad routes had declined with the expanded use of automobiles. Nevertheless, the community lingered. Around 1909, a new hotel and general store were built across from the station. And in the 1920s, a service station was built beside the tunnel portal to encourage visitors passing through by car. But the writing was on the wall.

Freight service to Laurel ended in 1920 and passenger service along the entire line was in freefall throughout the late 1920s and 1930s. By 1940, only 35 people still lived in the immediate area around Laurel station. The severe damage to the railroad line in February of that year led to the abandonment of the railroad route through the Santa Cruz Mountains and the formal closure of the train station on December 1, 1941. The tunnels on either side of the town were dismantled by H. A. Christie & Sons and subsequently dynamited by the Army Corps of Engineers in April 1942. Afterwards, Laurel residents converted the former tunnel to Glenwood into a water reservoir, which they continued to use until the 1989 Loma Prieta Earthquake. The school lasted until 1947, and the post office, which operated out of the former railroad depot, closed in July 1953. Many of the other buildings from the hamlet remained behind for nearly eighty years until Santa Cruz County finally demolished them in 1994 due to safety concerns. The foundations of these buildings still occupy a vacant lot beside the former railroad right-of-way, long since converted into a private driveway.

The historical significance of Laurel was documented on a plaque erected outside of the former service station, now a private residence, in September 1971 by the Santa Cruz County Bicentennial Commission. Its history also survives through the names of the roads emanating from its center: Laurel Road, Schulties Road, Morrell Mill Road, Tunnel Road, Redwood Lodge Road, and Stage Stop Way. Commuters on Highway 17 probably know the community best because of the notorious Laurel Curve, which has been the cause of many accidents since the highway first opened to traffic in 1940.

A couple in a buggy near Laurel, ca 1901. (*Santa Cruz Public Libraries*)

Cyanotype view of Laurel Station through the trees, 1891. (*Author's collection*)

Passengers waiting for a train outside Laurel Station, circa 1890. (*Randolph Brandt Collection, courtesy Jim Vail*)

Four views of Laurel Station looking west toward the tunnel to Glenwood, circa 1903. Each photograph shows the original South Pacific Coast Railroad depot with passengers and railroad staff milling around, flatcars on tracks (some with timber products loaded), and the railroad west portal of the tunnel in the background. Three of the photographs also include South Pacific Coast Railway boxcars. (*Above: Santa Cruz Public Libraries; below: Author's collection*)

(*Above and below: UC Santa Cruz*)

View of Laurel Station, circa 1895. (*Santa Cruz Museum of Art & History*)

A view of Laurel from inside the tunnel to Glenwood, circa 1900. (*Santa Cruz Museum of Art & History*)

Laurel, circa 1903. An empty flat car sits in front of a flatcar loaded with lumber, both cars attached to separate Southern Pacific Railroad boxcars. Piles of splitstuff are stacked along and between the tracks. (*UC Santa Cruz*)

Passengers waiting at Laurel Station while a flatcar loaded high with splitstuff sits on a nearby siding, circa 1903. (*History San José*)

Passengers waiting at Laurel as a freight train passes beside the station, circa 1903. Note the brakemen on top of the boxcar, the baby in the buggy, and the sign for the Wells-Fargo Express agency, located in the station. (*Author's collection*)

Laurel as viewed from inside the recently-upgraded tunnel to Glenwood, circa 1910. (*Edward Fenn*)

SIDETRACKED

Above: A Southern Pacific commuter train passing a boxcar at Laurel, 1913. (*Ginger Constantine Navarrete*)

Opposite: Another view of Laurel from inside the tunnel to Glenwood, circa 1910. (*Santa Cruz Museum of Art & History*)

The new tunnel portal at Laurel, 1909. This new portal, like those elsewhere along the line, supports standard-gauge trains and was reinforced against earthquakes by using Portland cement. Photo by George Besaw. (*Michael J. Semas*)

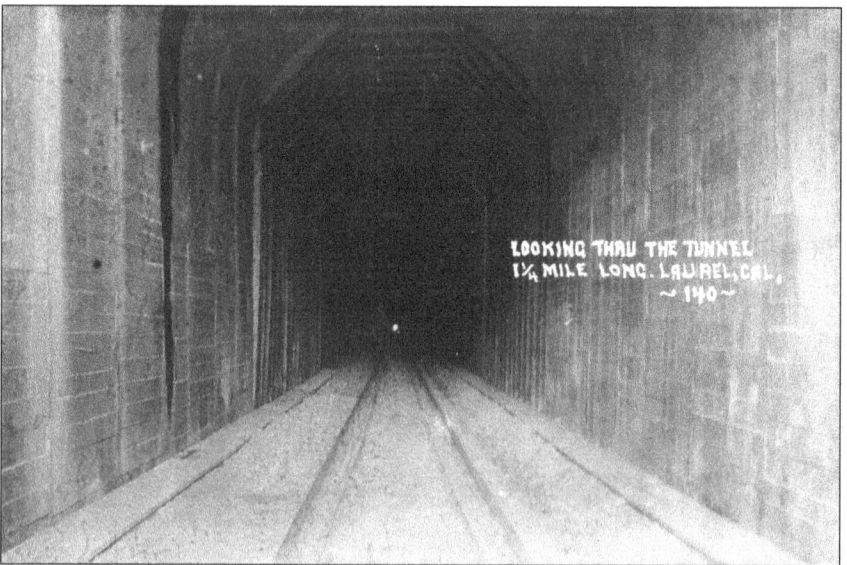

Looking through the tunnel to Glenwood, 1.25 miles away, 1909. Note the transition from concrete walls to timber framework. (*California State Library*)

Laurel resumed its life as a mill town after the 1906 Earthquake. The village expanded with the addition of a general store and hotel, which remained prominent features into the 1940s. (*Ronnie Trubek*)

In the mid-1910s, residents installed a stone name on the hill behind the store to welcome railroad passengers to Laurel. (*Santa Cruz Museum of Art & History*)

The general store at Laurel across from the railroad station, with a boxcar parked on a siding, 1909. Photo by George Besaw. (*Michael J. Semas*)

A distant view of Laurel, circa 1920. (*Santa Cruz Museum of Art & History*)

Gertrude Irene Lindsay and her brother at Laurel Station, circa 1913. (*Ginger Constantine Navarrete*)

A passenger train approaching Laurel Station with a Model T Ford parked in front of the general store, 1920s. (*Santa Cruz Museum of Art & History*)

A Model T Ford parked outside the Laurel store, 1920s. Probably taken the same day as the opposite photograph. The railroad station has been closed for several years. (*Santa Cruz Museum of Art & History*)

A Southern Pacific double-headed excursion train, probably a *Sun Tan Special*, passing through Laurel, 1939. Photograph by Wilbur C. Whittaker. (*Jim Vail*)

A man and a woman standing outside the shuttered Laurel depot, 1930s. (*Author's collection*)

Overgrown tracks beside the abandoned Laurel Station with the tunnel to Glenwood visible in the distance, 1939. Photograph by Wilbur C. Whittaker. (*Jim Vail*)

Laurel Station, functioning as the village's post office, sitting beside overgrown tracks, late 1939. (*Author's collection*)

A Southern Pacific passenger train crossing the Laurel–Schulties Road intersection before entering the tunnel to Glenwood, circa 1939. (*Santa Cruz Museum of Art & History*)

#22-M.P.L-G3.S-Laurel-View East at mud on road bed at west end Tunnel 2-4-9-40

Post-1940 storm survey photo of the right-of-way through Laurel, the west portal of the tunnel to Glenwood in the distance, April 3, 1940. (*Bruce MacGregor*)

H 21 M.P.L 63.4 Laurel View East at Side Wash 4-5-40

Post-1940 storm survey photos of the right-of-way in front of (above) and just to the east of (below) Laurel depot, April 9, 1940. (*Bruce MacGregor*)

8

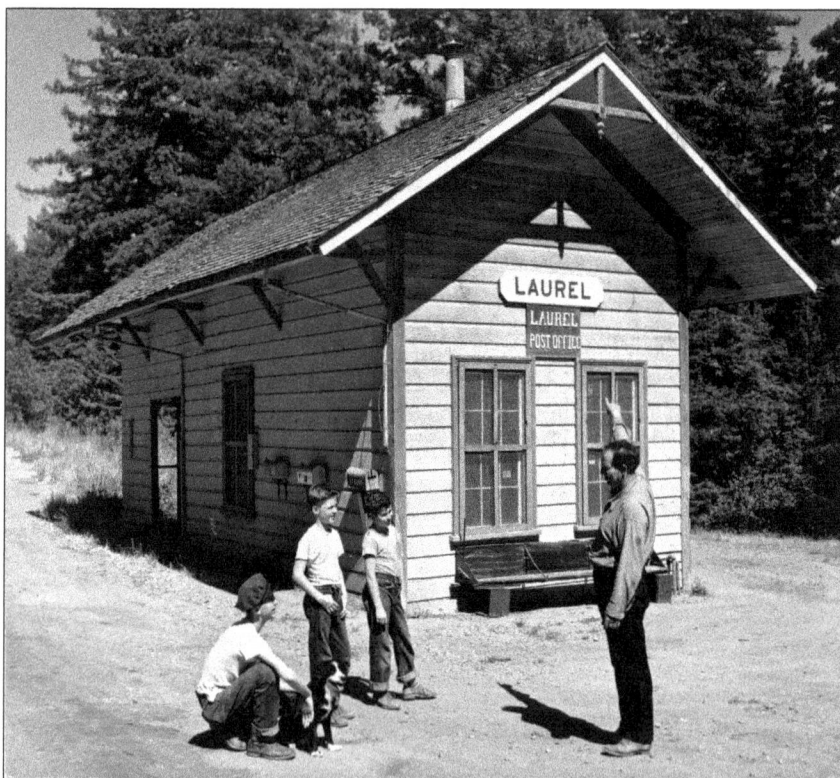

Three boys listening to a man talk about Laurel Station, August 1948. At this point, the station served as the settlement's post office. Photo by Ed Webber. (*UC Santa Cruz*)

Locals looking at damage to the Laurel service station and grocery following some accident or storm, circa 1945. The west portal of the abandoned tunnel to Glenwood is visible behind the building. (*Santa Cruz Museum of Art & History*)

The west portal of the tunnel to Glenwood, showing the cave-in with light showing through, June 23, 2011. Photo by Derek R. Whaley. (*Author's collection*)

The first Laurel mill nearing completion, September 16, 1900. (*Santa Cruz Museum of Art & History*)

Hihn's Mill

Laurel is undoubtedly one of the least known settlements in the Santa Cruz Mountains. It made little long-term impact within the greater region and left almost no lingering evidence of its existence except as a location on maps. While people do still live in and around the former village, their postal address is in Los Gatos and their location is simply unincorporated Santa Cruz County. For all intents and purposes, Laurel is a ghost town—a whisper of a bygone age. Yet from 1900 to 1906, it was the beating heart of Santa Cruz County's lumber industry.

The headwaters of the West Branch of Soquel Creek have had a long relationship with the logging industry. Frederick A. Hihn leased out various parts of Tract 16 of the former Rancho Soquel Augmentation to anyone who was willing to try their hand at cutting timber. Redwood and other trees cut from the area were instrumental in the construction of the South Pacific Coast Railroad and continued to play a part in its ongoing operation through the area. Mills breathed life into the upper Soquel Creek basin and ensured that it maintained a small population, especially through the summer months. But there were rarely enough people to sustain a healthy community.

Everything changed in January 1900. The F. A. Hihn Company had exhausted its reserves of timber along Gold Gulch south of Felton and needed a new source to harvest. The company had already cut all the usable timber from the Valencia Creek watershed, and its remaining acreage along the East Branch of Soquel Creek and up Bridge Creek near Aptos was too remote to profitably harvest. However, Hihn had convinced the South Pacific Coast Railroad to build its route directly through his Tract 16 in 1880. It was finally time to collect on this two-decade-old deal.

The company began to relocate its operations to Laurel in February 1900, with a shingle mill opening along the tracks before the end of the summer. Machinery for the mill was brought in by rail from Gold Gulch, while new timber structures were erected on site. The total cost of the facility was estimated to be $30,000. The mill opened in November with a capacity of 25,000 board feet of lumber produced per day. The company's goal for 1901 was to increase this to 45,000 board feet per day, the capacity it operated at on Gold Gulch. Near the lumber mill, a box mill was erected capable of producing 1,000 fruit boxes/day. A shingle mill was also built nearby which could produce 30,000 shingles, grape stakes, and other splitstuff per day.

Support facilities were built around the mill. To the north, at the confluence of Laurel and Burns Creeks, a broad millpond was formed, over which Hotel de Redwood Road crossed on a high bridge. Initially, logs were dragged to the pond using a combination of mules, horses, and steam donkey engines. Later, railcars brought the logs to the pond. To the south, a large lumberyard sprawled beside Soquel Creek, which was culverted through the mill grounds. In August 1901, construction was completed on a 1,600-foot-long narrow-gauge cable tramway that connected the lumberyard with the Southern Pacific tracks at Laurel. At the top of the grade beside the west portal of the tunnel to Glenwood, a warehouse was built that probably housed the disassembled remains of Hihn's Betsy Jane saddleback locomotive. The engine of the locomotive was attached to a steel drum around which a 1-inch-thick cable was wound. This was used to pull loaded flatcars up the incline to the railroad grade. At its steepest point, the incline achieved a 13% grade. No locomotive operated in the mill yard—cars were shuttled around the yard using mule or horse teams.

By summer 1902, over 100 people were employed at the mill in various capacities. Most of the workers were Italian and Irish, and Hihn even attempted to establish a Catholic church in Laurel to support their religious beliefs. Single men lived on site in two bunkhouses built between the mill and the cookhouse; married men lived with their families in cottages erected on the hillsides above Laurel. Seemingly overnight, Laurel became a much more substantial settlement and the focal point of a great logging enterprise. Timber products made at the mill were shipped throughout the Bay Area, with the Southern Pacific Railroad and the Western Union Telegraph Company some of the F. A. Hihn Company's biggest customers. An expansive freight yard was created beside Laurel station, with two long spurs adding 1,766 total feet of track to the station.

This initial mill operated near peak efficiency for over a year, but then disaster struck. On September 1, 1902, a fire broke out and destroyed virtually everything on the site. The cookhouse, bunkhouses, and mill office were the only structures to survive. Over 1,500,000 board feet of lumber burned in the inferno, costing the company thousands of dollars in lost revenue. Since the fire occurred so late in the season, the company decided not to rebuild until the next spring, after the end of the rainy season. The new facility opened in May 1903. It was capable of producing 50,000 board feet of lumber per day using an innovative new band saw. A new shingle mill was built nearby that could produce 50,000 board feet of splitstuff per day. Other support structures were also rebuilt, with everything operating at full capacity by summer. Unfortunately, no photographs seem to survive of this second mill.

Over three seasons, much of Tract 16 was logged and the hills became stripped of their redwoods. By February 1906, plans were in place to extend a logging road down the West Branch of Soquel Creek until it eventually reached Soquel. However, these plans came to an abrupt end in April, when the San Francisco Earthquake struck, briefly cutting off Laurel and the mill from the outside world. Even though rail service to Santa Cruz was restored by June 1906, the F. A. Hihn Company decided to relocate its operations to Kings Creek north of Boulder Creek. It was simply too expensive to ship from Laurel.

Local workers were loaned to the railroad to help it rebuild sections of the right-of-way between Los Gatos and Santa Cruz. In late 1907, the Summit Tunnel finally reopened and, over the winter, crews standard gauged the track to Laurel. At the same time, the Hihn Company upgraded the cable incline to standard gauge and replaced its rolling stock with larger flatcars. Disappointingly for the milling company, the Panic of 1907 had depressed the lumber market, and made reopening the mill at Laurel problematic. In May 1908, the company hoped to buck the trend and reopened with a full complement of workers. But the gamble did not pay off and the mill closed only a month later. Half the crew was fired and the other half went back to Kings Creek. Contrary to popular belief, the Laurel mill did not provide any large quantity of wood to the rebuild of San Francisco in the three years immediately after the earthquake. Most of the lumber used to rebuild the city came from the mill on Kings Creek and the Loma Prieta Lumber Company's mill on Little Creek north of Davenport.

In 1909, the route through the mountains opened to standard-gauge traffic and the Laurel mill resumed normal operations. For the next five years, the mill operated at a variable capacity. Over the precious decade, most of Soquel Creek south of the mill had been logged, but areas above the town to the northwesternmost corner of Tract 16 remained untouched. Logging operations were scaled back, with the shingle mill operating year-round but the lumber mill only operating a few months each year. Lumber from Laurel was used to build the Casa del Rey Hotel in Santa Cruz in 1911, but most of the lumber went to the Hihn–Hammond planing mill and lumber yard in Santa Cruz. The last big push at the mill occurred in 1913, after which the company wound down operations until closing completely around the time that the United States entered World War I in April 1917. By this point, most of the company's focus was on the remaining tracts of timber available at the headwaters of Bridge Creek in today's Forest of Nisene Marks State Park.

The site of the mill went through numerous permutations in the years after the mill closed. In 1915, the lumberyard was converted into a small orchard, but the business failed to produce commercially viable crops. During this time, two cabins were constructed by repurposing old structural materials found in the old millpond's dam and elsewhere on site. In 1943, the site was purchased by Alan Medlen, who set up a foster home for boys. They built a swimming pool and campground, while also expanding the old company office, cookhouse, and two cabins. By the 1960s, the location had been upgraded into a small retreat and massage school known as Getting In Touch. A second swimming pool and a jacuzzi were added and all the buildings were upgraded and modernized. However, damage from the 1982 winter storms forced the retreat to shut its doors. After repairs were made, the location briefly became a nudist resort run by Nancy Penny, accessible via ropes and ladders installed along Redwood Lodge Road. But that business went bankrupt a few years later. Eventually, in 1991, Esther Seehof and Bob Kundus purchased the property and reopened it as Laurel Mill Lodge, an event and wedding venue. They sold the resort to a private party around 2020.

A view up the cable incline to the Hihn mill looking toward Laurel, circa 1901. Note the cable sitting to the left of the tracks and the telegraph wire above it. Standard gauge ties were used to make the transition to broad gauge width easier. (*Evelyn Bowles Collection, Santa Cruz Museum of Art & History*)

Down the cable incline to the Hihn mill, possibly after a winter storm, circa 1901. The steep 13% grade is apparent at this angle and the cable can be seen lying across the tracks. (*Evelyn Bowles Collection, Santa Cruz Museum of Art & History*)

A view down the incline following its upgrade to standard-gauge, circa 1910. Note the car loaded with splitstuff on the track in the distance. (*George Pepper*)

A flatcar full of lumber being pulled up the incline cableway from the Hihn mill, circa 1902. (*Santa Cruz Museum of Art & History*)

Final approach to the end of the incline, with the lumberyard to the left and several mill buildings in the distance, circa 1901. (*Evelyn Bowles Collection, Santa Cruz Museum of Art & History*)

Trackage beyond the end of the incline above the West Branch of Soquel Creek, circa 1901. (*Evelyn Bowles Collection, Santa Cruz Museum of Art & History*)

The mill office and a warehouse across from tall stacks of lumber, circa 1901. (*Evelyn Bowles Collection, Santa Cruz Museum of Art & History*)

The mill office, cookhouse, and warehouse across the tracks from the lumberyard, circa 1901. (*Evelyn Bowles Collection, Santa Cruz Museum of Art & History*)

Looking across the lumberyard toward the mill, with workers loading flatcars, circa 1901. (*Evelyn Bowles Collection, Santa Cruz Museum of Art & History*)

Postcard of workers posing outside the cookhouse of the second mill, circa 1910. (*Art Goddard Collection, UC Santa Cruz*)

Tramway tracks running through the center of the lumberyard with tall stacks of lumber on either side and the mill in the distance, circa 1901. (*Evelyn Bowles Collection, Santa Cruz Museum of Art & History*)

The Laurel mill with the millpond in the foreground and a blacksmith shop to the left, circa 1901. (*Evelyn Bowles Collection, Santa Cruz Museum of Art & History*)

A worker standing beside the band saw inside the Laurel mill, circa 1903. (*Santa Cruz Museum of Art & History*)

View of the mill from above Hotel de Redwood Road, which wraps around the back of it, circa 1902. (*UC Santa Cruz*)

The Hotel de Redwood Road bridge over the back of the millpond, circa 1901. (*Evelyn Bowles Collection, Santa Cruz Museum of Art & History*)

A skidroad passes beside the millpond and continues up Burns Creek toward the Southern Pacific Railroad's Summit Tunnel. This photograph was likely taken looking upstream from atop the Hotel de Redwood Road bridge, circa 1901. (*Evelyn Bowles Collection, Santa Cruz Museum of Art & History*)

A horse team hauling a log on a wagon near Laurel, 1911. (*UC Santa Cruz*)

A shed to protect a bull donkey engine that dragged logs by cable along a skidroad to the millpond, circa 1901. (*Evelyn Bowles Collection, Santa Cruz Museum of Art & History*)

View across the tracks to C. E. Draper's General Store on the Glenwood Highway, circa 1930. (*Santa Cruz Museum of Art & History*)

GLENWOOD

Eighty years before the arrival of the South Pacific Coast Railroad workers to the Bean Creek valley, the Franciscan Trail between Santa Cruz and Santa Clara passed through the verdant vale. Twenty years before, Mountain Charlie McKiernan's Santa Cruz Turnpike was built, paralleling Bean Creek for some of its distance. Early settlers such as John M. Bean had planted orchards and vineyards on the hillsides, and the Glenwood Magnetic Springs attracted people seeking treatments for ailments from across the Central Coast. However, beyond this, not much can be said about Glenwood prior to the arrival of the railroad.

The community's purported patriarch, Charles Christopher Martin, only permanently moved to the area around 1870. His influence was substantial compared to that of his neighbors, but there was only the barest trace of a village in the valley when crews began work on the railroad in 1878. Even the story of how the community got its name is apocryphal. According to Martin's great-granddaughter, Margaret Koch, the settlement was originally named Bean Hollow before Martin's largess led to it being renamed Martinsville. There is no primary evidence for either of these names, though. Later, as the story goes, Martin changed the name to Glenwood following the recommendation of a Scottish friend who thought it was a more descriptive name for the valley. The major problem with this tale is that the first use of the poetic name was actually by Andrew J. Haight when he opened Glenwood House at the popular Magnetic Springs in April 1877. This name was then adopted by the railroad to associate the station with the resort.

Regardless of the origins of Glenwood, it was Martin who ensured that the mountain vale was not left off the route of the South Pacific Coast Railroad. As an investor, he had influence over many local businesses and wanted to see them prosper for personal and collective reasons. Therefore, he joined with Frederick Hihn and other interested parties to petition the railroad to direct its line through the Bean Creek valley. Martin granted the railroad the entirety of its right-of-way through the valley, a stretch of track over a mile long. In addition, he gave permission to build tunnels at either end of this section. Tunnel No. 3, which went in the direction of Highland, had its east portal at the north end of the valley, while Tunnel No. 4, to the Zayante Creek valley, was below McKiernan Toll Road. Martin allowed work crews to camp on his sprawling meadow, and he donated the flattest section of his land for the depot and railyard.

Glenwood's depot, which opened with the rail line in May 1880, initially consisted of two buildings: a passenger office and a freight shed. The office was a narrow structure measuring 12 feet deep by about 40 feet long, while the shed was similarly-sized and raised with a long platform along the track side. Around 1895, these two structures were joined together and a bay window was added to the office to serve as a ticket window. Glenwood marked the southern end of an eight-mile section of track where there were no passing sidings. To avoid collisions, the railroad put in a track management system between Alma and Glenwood to ensure that only one train was ever on this section at a time. All westbound trains had to stop to collect a token from the Glenwood office. This token was then turned in to the agent at Alma, who then delivered it to the next eastbound train. When the eastbound train arrived at Glenwood, the conductor handed the token back to the station agent. This system was eventually replaced with automated block signals after the 1906 San Francisco Earthquake.

Glenwood served an important role in the South Pacific Coast Railroad's freight operations over the Santa Cruz Mountains. The station sat at the top of the steepest section of the railroad grade. Locomotives running on sections of the track above Zayante Creek were forced to shuttle short trains of laden lumber cars to Glenwood in order to assemble a full-length train. As a result, a turntable was installed in August 1883 at the western end of its freight yard and several sidings and spurs were installed which totaled a combined 2,705 feet in length. Once assembled, trains consisting of several dozen cars headed out to the Bay Area. A permanent watchman oversaw freight transfer operations at

Glenwood throughout the 1880s to ensure cars were moved safely, especially since much of the shuttling and assembly was done at night. This complex arrangement endured into the early 1890s, when more efficient Southern Pacific locomotives were able to overcome the steep grade and make the entire run between Felton and San José without stopping.

Millions of board feet of lumber from the mills of the San Lorenzo and Zayante Valleys passed through Glenwood, putting the village on the map. Martin founded the Glenwood Post Office, initially running it out of his home, on August 23, 1880. In 1886, he sponsored the construction of a public school, which suggests that a sufficient number of year-round residents had moved into the area. By 1890, Martin had erected a large general store directly across from the railroad depot. On either side of Bean Creek, vineyards and orchards stretched to the hilltops, the produce and products shipped out from the station. And the local resort industry expanded with the openings of Summer Home Farm, Mount Pleasant Farm, Glenwood Hotel, Villa Fontenay, and Gibbs Resort. Glenwood thrived during the summer months, when hundreds of vacationers camped and relaxed in the woods and meadows, frequently visiting the station to welcome friends and loved ones or the general store to buy provisions and send postcards back home.

The San Francisco Earthquake in 1906 only briefly interrupted the community's success. Indeed, the increased remoteness of Glenwood was marketed as a perk, since it meant less disturbance from the outside world. Nevertheless, accessing Glenwood became an arduous journey with travelers having to take the train south from San José, up the Pajaro Valley, up the coast to Santa Cruz, and then up the San Lorenzo Valley. Work restoring and upgrading the damaged Summit Tunnel was completed in late 1907, but the financial panic of that year delayed the standard-gauging of Tunnel No. 3. As a result, the tracks to Glenwood were standard gauged but the tunnel was not. The old turntable, largely unused for a decade, was reinforced to turn standard-gauge locomotives, but it sagged dangerously low due to the increased weight. As soon as the upgrading of the tunnel was finally completed in March 1909, the turntable was removed and the pit filled.

Along with the other portals, the west portal of Tunnel No. 3 was enlarged to support standard-gauge trains and rebuilt in concrete, with a short brick ceiling to better support the sandy embankment above it. As with the previous iteration of the tunnel, the interior was only lightly timbered as the mountain itself was relatively stable. In 1910, lighting was also installed inside, possibly to make it easier to maintain. In the late 1910s, the Glenwood Highway was installed directly over the west portal, pulling the hillside back from the tunnel while also creating an even steeper rock face. The interior was likely reinforced at the same time, though no photographs exist to compare.

The standard gauging of the tracks through Glenwood had a contradictory impact on the settlement. A broader gauge meant that heavier-duty trains could transport more people in comfort to Glenwood, which is indeed what occurred in the early years of the 1910s. However, freight revenue fell almost to zero during this period and never recovered, with many of the vineyards and orchards either shutting down or shifting to using trucks to transport goods. Any vineyards that were still shipping wine by train until 1920 were suddenly out of business when Prohibition set in. As a result, most of the newly-installed sidings and spurs were abandoned and left to rot. Thus, even as rider experience improved and capacity along the line increased, the commercial function of the line declined. With respect to Glenwood, the railroad became exclusively a passenger affair.

Charles Martin was unphased by the collapse of freight revenue from his village. The resort industry was thriving and people clearly wanted to vacation there. Thus, when the California government finally decided to establish a steel-reinforced concrete highway through the Santa Cruz Mountains, Martin not only petitioned them to route the road through Glenwood, but he even did the survey work for them. He hoped that the increase in private vehicular traffic through the hamlet would increase patronage at the resorts and perhaps even return industry to the valley. Construction of the military-grade road began around 1916 and continued throughout World War I. When it was completed to Glenwood in 1919, a very aged Martin placed his feet and initials in the cement near his hotel. A new service station opened to cater to passing motorists, and the general store was enlarged.

The Glenwood Highway, as it was known, was completed in 1920 and the traffic certainly came, but most of it continued on without stopping. People wanted to spend the weekend at the Santa Cruz Beach Boardwalk, the California Redwood Park, or Welch's Big Trees. Their fast-paced, teetotalling lifestyles no longer left time to spend entire summers lounging on mountain brooksides reading books and playing cards until the mosquitos came out. Martin's last gamble marked the end of an era for Glenwood, though he did not live to see it. Charles Martin died on December 30, 1920.

By the end of the 1920s, all of the local resorts were closed or had been repurposed. Without freight customers, Southern Pacific abandoned its freight agency in 1927. A small number of local commuters still used the passenger service, and a trickle of vacationers continued to visit the hamlet of Glenwood in the summer months. However, in 1934, vehicular traffic was diverted to a new road—Highway 5 (now Highway 17)—that bypassed Glenwood. As a result, the general store and gas station both closed. Residents must have moved away as well, since Southern Pacific decided to close its passenger office on August 16, 1939 due to a lack of patronage. The 196 residents of the Glenwood basin could still catch the daily commuter train at Glenwood, but they had to flag it down. Thus, the de facto closure of the railroad route through the mountains in February 1940 due to storm damage had surprisingly little impact on the community. Like Laurel one long tunnel away, Glenwood had already been defeated.

Over the next two years, the depot was torn down, the trackage removed, and the tunnels dynamited. All of the railroad property within the Glenwood basin either reverted to its previous owners or was sold. Some of the community's old infrastructure lingered into the 1950s. Glenwood School welcomed new students until the end of the 1950 school year, after which the district was merged with Scotts Valley and the schoolhouse shut down. The Glenwood Post Office, probably still used by the Dominican Sisters and the Camp Redwood Glen boys, finally shut its doors on April 30, 1954. Its last postmaster was Margaret Koch, great-granddaughter of Charles Martin. In 1972, the Glenwood Highway was paved with asphalt and Martin's markings disappeared.

People still live in Glenwood today—in fact it has a larger population now than it ever had in the age of the railroad—but almost nothing of that era survives. The railroad right-of-way is now driveways and fields. The depot site is a small vineyard. Only the tunnel portal survives, albeit hidden from view and public awareness, appearing as simply a half bridge north of the former village center. On June 22, 1950, in commemoration of the community that once was, Glenwood was declared a State Registered Landmark and a plaque was erected at the former depot site. It still sits there, an old wagon wheel leaning against it, an insufficient memorial to a bygone time.

Probably the earliest photograph of Glenwood Station, showing the depot and a bridge over Bean Creek, but no other buildings, circa 1880. A passenger train is preparing to leave for Santa Cruz. (*Santa Cruz Museum of Art & History*)

A train leaving Glenwood and heading into the tunnel to Laurel, with stacks of lumber beside parked boxcars, circa 1914. (*UC Santa Cruz*)

The Santa Cruz commuter train entering Glenwood from the tunnel, 1919. (*Author's collection*)

A glimpse of Glenwood looking along the new highway toward the train station, with two contractors in the foreground, circa 1914. (*Sourisseau Academy*)

View from about the same location showing a South Pacific Coast Railway passenger train beside Glenwood Station with a long freight train beside it preparing to head out, circa 1890. (*Mount Hermon Association*)

View of Glenwood Station from the northwest with a passenger train having just departed for Santa Cruz, circa 1900. (*Edward Fenn*)

A passenger train parked outside Glenwood Station on a snowy day, circa 1930. (*Jeff Escott*)

Glenwood Station with a handcar on a siding, circa 1890. (*Author's collection*)

Glenwood Station, circa 1890. (*Santa Cruz Museum of Art & History*)

A passenger train parked outside Glenwood Station with people standing on a flatcar parked beside the platform, circa 1900. (*Author's collection*)

A boxcar sitting beside the freight platform with a passenger car parked on a spur in the distance, circa 1910. The station has recently been remodeled with the addition of a bay window. It has also been extended to connect with the adjacent freight shed. (*Jim Cirner*)

Cyanotype of Glenwood Station looking north, 1891. Note the turntable at left used to turn locomotives back to Felton for hauling lumber. (*Author's collection*)

Glenwood Station from just beyond the southern end of the yard, circa 1900. (*California State Library*)

A child standing between tracks within the Glenwood Station rail yard, circa 1905. (*Santa Cruz Museum of Art & History*)

A Ford Model T parked outside the Glenwood Post Office, service station, and general store, circa 1918. (*UC Santa Cruz*)

Overgrown tracks at Glenwood with miscellaneous rolling stock parked on a siding in the distance, late 1930s. (*Author's collection*)

Glenwood Station after the agency closed, July 9, 1939. A ballast car sits on the overgrown siding beside the platform. Photograph by Wilbur C. Whittaker. (*Jim Vail*)

SIDETRACKED

Glenwood Station following abandonment, shortly after the depot was removed, May 1940. (*Harold Van Gorder, Santa Cruz Museum of Art & History*)

Contract crew for Marshall & Foss posing above the east portal of the Glenwood Tunnel as they ride into Glenwood to begin work on the Glenwood Highway, circa 1914. (*Margaret Koch Collection, Santa Cruz Museum of Art & History*)

View looking down at the entrance to the abandoned east portal of the tunnel to Laurel, date unknown. (*Ralph Leidy*)

Glenwood School just beyond the abandoned east portal of the tunnel to Laurel, located below the metal railings on Glenwood Highway in the foreground, 1940s. (*Santa Cruz Museum of Art & History*)

The meadow where the Glenwood Hotel once stood, May 5, 2011. Photo by Derek R. Whaley. (*Author's collection*)

The westbound Southern Pacific commuter train approaching Clems Station, where two passengers wait to board, circa 1910. The rustic nature of this remote station shelter was unique among those along the mountain route. (*Santa Cruz Museum of Art & History*)

CLEMS

Glenwood was situated at the northeastern end of the South Pacific Coast Railroad's right-of-way along Bean Creek, but it was not the only station in the valley. A little over a mile to the southwest sat unassuming and oft-overlooked Clems.

Although the distance from Glenwood to Clems was not great, the route between them crossed some difficult terrain. The railroad crossed to the west bank of Bean Creek via a short but high trestle located just south of the Glenwood station yard. During standard-gauging, this was turned into a concrete culvert. South of the bridge, the right-of-way was wide enough to support a long siding, presumably used to hold lumber cars awaiting assembly. Once the track turned east, however, the right-of-way narrowed severely and continued pressed against the western hillside until reaching the Mountain Charlie Tunnel. In the late 1870s, Chinese workers carved out and dynamited a railroad grade directly into the hillside, but the railroad still had to install multiple half-bridges to ensure an even and stable grade. Although no photographs of these half-bridges survive, their remains can be easily seen across Bean Creek along the 0.5-mile-long portion of Glenwood Drive between Stonewood Drive and Tadstone Lane.

At the westernmost end of this stretch of right-of-way, the South Pacific Coast Railroad encountered a sandstone hillside atop which ran the McKiernan Toll Road, now Mountain Charlie Road. It was vital for the railroad to reach the Zayante Creek basin beyond; however, the task was not easy. The short bore through the narrow ridge required extensive redwood bracing to ensure that the passage would remain intact. The contract for construction was given to Osborn & Company, which completed the tunnel on Christmas Eve 1878. The firm clearly knew what it was doing. No known incident ever occurred in the tunnel, and it survived forest fires, winter storms, and the 1906 Earthquake.

Near the west portal of the tunnel, E. A. Clem & Company took advantage of the close proximity of the railroad line and purchased a tract of timberland for $1,500 in July 1881. Thirty lumbermen were promptly hired and a small mill erected somewhere nearby, probably in the vicinity of today's Glenwood Drive just before the bridge over Bean Creek. The South Pacific Coast Railroad responded to this new freight customer by installing a short, 186-foot-long spur to the mill. Initially, one of Clem's partners, D. Gardiner, ran the mill while Clem and J. E. Doolittle operated a retail lumber yard in Oakland. However, Gardiner committed suicide in 1882 after embezzling money from the company. This quickly led to the collapse of the lumber firm. Nevertheless, the station lingered on.

When the Southern Pacific Railroad took over in 1887, "Tunnel No. 4 (Clems)" was added as a stop in agency books. It retained this designation until the closure of the line in 1940, suggesting that the railroad considered the station first and foremost home to the tunnel's maintenance car. At some point in mid-1897, following a petition from the Haesters, who ran nearby Summer Home Farm, Clems was added to Southern Pacific Railroad employee timetables as a flag stop. It was likely the Haesters who erected the small, open-air, untreated log passenger shelter that sat between the tracks and the hillside. This shelter was located at the end of the accessway that linked the railroad to the county road along Bean Creek. Today, this accessway is a private driveway with a gate to keep out trespassers. Clem's Switch, as newspapers called the station, did not prove popular with new arrivals to Summer Home Farm, but it was likely used by long-term vacationers and residents.

In 1907, the Santa Cruz Portland Cement Company of Davenport began quarrying clay at a site near Clems and it used the old narrow-gauge spur for shipments. The clay in the area, which was also found on the other side of the ridge near Tank Siding, was highly desired for use in the company's premium cement products. When the company came under new ownership in 1908, the former owner, William J. Dingee, wished to keep the Clems quarry for his own use, a suggestion that the new owners refused. The clay was simply too valuable. By 1909, the quarry was operating at peak efficiency with fifty employees mining in the hills. Clay for shipment was hauled to the spur in front of the west portal of the tunnel and then loaded onto waiting freight cars. In 1915, this spur was also briefly used by contractors rebuilding the road bridges over Bean Creek, who received materials by train and probably unloaded them at the site of the former mill. The spur disappeared from timetables in late 1916, suggesting that the cement company loaded its clay directly onto cars parked on the mainline after this point.

The Mountain Charlie Tunnel was greatly enlarged in 1908 as part of the project to standard gauge the entire mountain route. The interior was widened, with the entire support structure replaced with more evenly-spaced redwood bents and beams. The sandstone walls and ceiling had proven remarkably stable, so Southern Pacific decided fewer support beams were required. Outside, new concrete portals were erected, both of identical design with tall concrete buttresses to ensure the portals remained upright. Because of the remoteness of the tunnels and the steep, sandy hillsides above them, no railings were installed above the portals.

Not long after the route through the mountains reopened, the station shelter at Clems was replaced. Gone was the rustic shelter shoved against the hillside. In its place was installed a standard prefabricated wood box shelter similar to those found at Zayante, Olympia, Eccles, and elsewhere in the Santa Cruz Mountains. This new shelter was probably situated on the creek side of the tracks, since that would be more accessible to passengers and would not require people to cross the tracks.

Clems transitioned to being an on-demand stop beginning around September 1931. This may have been after the Santa Cruz Portland Cement Company wrapped up operations at its quarry. Abandoned equipment from the operation still littered the area outside the west portal of the tunnel when the line closed in 1940. Regular passenger service to the station also ended at this time, though the station remained on the books until the formal abandonment of the line in November 1940. At the time of the line's closure, the Interstate Commerce Commission reported that only four people lived within the vicinity of Clems station, clearly an insufficient number to justify its continued existence. The shelter was removed in 1941 and its ultimate fate is unknown.

After the line was closed and the Mountain Charlie Tunnel unceremoniously dynamited at each end in 1942, the east portal of the tunnel began its second life as a destination for backwoods explorers. The explosion had inadvertently caused the sandstone ceiling to weaken within the tunnel. By the 1970s, a hole had appeared above a portion of the tunnel, accessible to people who climbed the hillside behind the east portal. Over the years, this hole enlarged until the entire right-of-way within the tunnel was accessible to daring explorers. People who have explored the interior have found that much of it remains intact, with large sandstone rocks scattered throughout and fallen bents and beams on the floor, but the walls and ceiling otherwise still holding firm.

A long section of double track south of Glenwood, with children crossing the tracks in the mid-distance, circa 1890. Note the vineyards on the hillside at left and the distinctive trees in the distance. (*Santa Cruz Museum of Art & History*)

Standard-gauge track in the forest near Glenwood Cut-off, circa 1920s. (*Margaret Koch Collection, Santa Cruz Museum of Art & History*)

Two photographs of a derailed hopper car on the tracks between Glenwood and Clems, 1930s. A man inspects the wreck in the photo above, while grass grows along the decreasingly maintained tracks. (*Margaret Koch Collection, Santa Cruz Museum of Art & History*)

A South Pacific Coast Railway train coming around the corner into Clems, 1898. (*Bruce MacGregor*)

A class, possibly from Boulder Creek School, posing for the camera outside the west portal of the tunnel under Mountain Charlie Road, circa 1890. Photo by Herb Martin. (*UC Santa Cruz*)

A woman standing outside the west portal of the Mountain Charlie tunnel shortly after the mountain route closed, circa summer 1940. (*Margaret Koch Collection, Santa Cruz Museum of Art & History*)

Post-1940 storm survey photo of the right-of-way in front of the west portal of the Mountain Charlie tunnel, March 1, 1940. (*Bruce MacGregor*)

The partially buried remains of the west portal of the Mountain Charlie tunnel, May 5, 2011. Photo by Derek R. Whaley. (*Author's collection*)

Sign beside the Glenwood Store advertising the many resorts located in and around the Bean Creek basin, circa 1902. (*Michael Maslan*)

A large group of picnickers wandering away from an excursion train parked at Glenwood, circa 1890. Most are walking in the direction of Bean Creek and Charles C. Martin's Glenwood Park picnic grounds. (*Gil Pennington*)

Mountain Resorts

The Santa Cruz Mountains have long been the haunt of adventurers, rogues, and all manner of frontierspeople. However, the completion of the San Francisco & San Jose Railroad in the 1860s brought the mountains closer to civilization than ever before, and as toll roads wound their way to the headwaters of Soquel, Bean, and Branciforte Creeks, pleasure-seekers followed. This evolution of the mountains from a howling wilderness to a playland of the Bay Area elite was accelerated by the arrival of the South Pacific Coast Railroad in 1880, which suddenly brought tourists directly to the picturesque glens and groves deep in the mountains.

From the 1880s to the 1920s, summers in the Santa Cruz Mountains were dominated by all-night parties, weekend picnic excursions, and mountain activities such as fishing, hunting, and swimming. San Francisco bankers bumped shoulders with rural farmers, reflecting an unspoken tug-of-war between local industry and recreation, with some bold resort owners attempting to profit from both. Throughout this period, seven resorts of note sprang up in the Laurel and Glenwood areas to cater to stagecoach and railroad customers.

Hotel de Redwood & Redwood Lodge (1870 – 1953)

An important waystation along the Soquel Turnpike (Soquel–San José Road), Hotel de Redwoods was the first resort built in the Summit area and was located above the headwaters of Soquel Creek. Erected in 1851, possibly by Edwin Bowker, it originally served as a combination home, general store, and hostelry for passing travelers. By 1870, the 'Hotel de Redwoods' had emerged as a unique experience for visitors since parts of the complex were constructed out of living portions of redwood trees, as well as repurposed tree stumps. Residents of the hotel enjoyed the adjacent Hester's Sulphur Springs—also operated by Bowker—and went hunting in the woods or fishing along Soquel Creek.

A post office under the management of Eugene F. West was established here on June 3, 1879. Operating under the abbreviated name Deredwood, it remained until October 16, 1882, when it relocated to Highland (later Laurel). Part of the reason for this relocation was the anticipated completion of the road between the hotel and Highland Station in 1885, which made the distance between the two locations only two miles. It was around this time that the resort was unpluralized to Hotel de Redwood.

With the arrival of the railroad, interest in the resort skyrocketed. Capt. Myron S. Cox, seeing its potential, purchased the hotel in 1884 and completely renovated it. He added a new two-story hotel building with ten guest rooms and a balcony. The following March, the entire complex burned down. Cox immediately rebuilt the hotel and by summer 1886, it could support 110 people between the new primary structure and the adjacent tents and cabins. Arthur P. Cox, son of Myron, took over management of the resort briefly, probably from 1901 to 1904. He operated the resort under the name Redwood Lodge, a name that returned periodically throughout its existence.

For the summer 1905 season, the Coxes hired Mr. and Mrs. A. J. Waltz to run the hotel. Their experience must have been favorable since they appear to have purchased the resort on April 1, 1906. Their timing was unfortunate since the San Francisco Earthquake struck less than three weeks later, severely damaging the property. Nonetheless, they rebuilt the main hotel and built several new outbuildings, and they continued to operate the hotel for decades. They turned the area around Hotel de Redwood into a small town, adding a general store, cottage city, and gas station for passing automobiles.

The end of the rail line and the completion of Highway 17, both in 1940, largely contributed to the closure of Santa Cruz County's oldest resort. When precisely the resort closed is unclear, but by 1949 it was in the hands of Pat Fitzgerald. The ageing hotel struggled through World War II and the early 1950s before succumbing to a massive fire in 1953. Nothing of this century-old resort remains except a concrete gas pumping island and a place name on maps.

Two stereographs showing a stage coach full of passengers arriving at the Hotel de Redwood, circa 1870s. (*California State Library*)

The entrance to the Hotel de Redwood, circa 1900. (*Jim Cirner*)

Hotel de Redwood,
SANTA CRUZ MOUNTAINS.

One of the most romantic and healthful resorts in the mountains. Fine water, with Iron and Sulphur springs. Rates, $8 per week up. Return tickets from San Francisco, $2.50, good for three months. For particulars, address,

M. S. COX,
Laurel Station, Santa Cruz Co., Cal.

Advertisement for the Hotel de Redwood, 1886–1900. (*Author's collection*)

The wrap-around cover to a promotional brochure for Arthur P. Cox's Redwood Lodge, 1901–1904. (*History San José*)

Glenwood Magnetic Springs (1872 – 1913)

The first purpose-built hotel in the Glenwood area was established in September 1872 on Charles Fisk's ranch on the northern slope of Vine Hill, about three miles from the McKiernan Toll Road. John Morrow's design for the 40' by 40' two-story hotel included eighteen guest rooms, a kitchen and dining room, workers' rooms, and communal spaces. The main appeal of the resort was its 'magnetic' springs, a tributary of Carbonera Creek with a high iron content that was used in various ways in the hope of treating diseases and improving general health and wellbeing. In addition to building his resort, which was attended year-round, Fisk planted grape vines to support the burgeoning wine industry.

In April 1877, the resort was taken over by Andrew J. Haight, a San Francisco jeweler and hotelier. He named the resort Glenwood Magnetic Springs, though he also called it the Glenwood House at the Magnetic Springs. The house may have been named after Glenwood, New York, a small community outside of Buffalo near where Haight grew up. The latter name may have been chosen in re-

Series of stereographs of Glenwood Magnetic Springs in the Vine Hill district.

Photographed by the studio of Carleton Watkins, 1882. (*California State Library*)

sponse to a short-lived rival on Bean Creek, DeWolf's Magnetic Springs, which appeared in 1875 and disappeared the next year. Under Haight's management, the 210-acre property became host to several cottages and outbuildings totalling 40 rooms for visitors. Haight also added tennis courts and a broad veranda for covered lounging. Orchards were planted to accompany the vineyard, combined covering over 50 acres, while hunting, fishing, and other outdoor activities were encouraged in the remainder of the property.

When the South Pacific Coast Railroad route opened in May 1880, Glenwood Magnetic Springs was an advertised destination for vacationers. It was the popularity of this resort that made Glenwood an early tourist destination. Visitors arrived at the hotel via a special horse-drawn bus that shuttled people the three miles from the train station. It was common for people suffering various ailments to remain at the resort all summer, while its close proximity to

Glenwood—only four miles—meant that businessmen could commute to San Francisco on weekdays and then relax at the resort with their families on weekends. This pattern of summer vacationing became common to all resorts in the Santa Cruz Mountains until the arrival of the automobile.

The property passed through a variety of proprietors and owners over the years. Charles A. Hubert and John N. Luff took over the Magnetic Springs on July 1, 1882. At the end of that summer season, they renovated the hotel and added a billiards room and a bowling alley. Luff bought out Hubert's interest in July 1883 and ran the resort himself afterwards. An unknown owner in 1886 renamed the resort Glenwood Mountain Home in 1886, a name that did not stick and became associated with the hotel building rather than the resort as a whole. In May 1890, William T. Halliday sold the resort to John C. Bedell, who in turn sold it to Catherine Lindsay in June. Lindsay ran the hotel for four summers before it passed into the hands of Frank McLaughlin in 1894, who renamed the resort Santa Maria Magnetic Springs. This name did not last the year. Emanuel H. Lyon took over in 1895 and hired J. P. Stockwell to manage the property. At the end of the year, Lyon offered to sell the property back to Lindsay. Catherine and Joseph Lindsay ran the hotel for three seasons before selling it to Lajos V. and Annie G. Perhacs in October 1898.

Less than a year after the Perhacs bought the property, a fire swept through the Vine Hill district and burned the hotel to the ground. In response, Lajos incorporated the Magnetic Springs Company on March 3, 1900, leading a group of five other men who together sought to rebuild the hotel as a deluxe 70-room building. Their vision was bold, but their finances were lacking. The firm defaulted on its mortgage and the entire property was sold at auction in June 1901 to Provident Mutual Building Loan Association. Dr. Oliver H. Simons acquired the property at some point in 1902, though it is unclear if he ran the resort during this time. Simons died unexpectedly in his bed in August 1903, prompting yet another change in ownership.

In December 1904, Col. C. L. Webb purchased the property with the intention of turning it into a private home, farm, and vineyard. He planned to spend $20,000 to erect a mid-sized country mansion, which he later named Burnau Villa. The estate appears to have survived the earthquake, as well as a large fire in October 1906, undamaged. Webb died in January 1907, but not before transferring the estate to Ella E. Webb. In 1910, Ella reopened the Magnetic Springs to summer visitors, though she emphasized an exclusion of Jews from the premises, a reflection of growing anti-Semitism at the time.

As with other nearby resorts, the increased popularity of the automobile combined with the start of World War I led to the closure of Glenwood Magnetic Springs. Webb stopped advertising after the 1912 summer season, and no resident lists are provided in newspapers after 1913. Ella later gifted the property to her relative, Mabel Burnau Webb, in 1930. Prohibition in the 1920s ended the wine industry in the region, further deflating the local resort industry. At some later point, Burnau Villa and all of its outbuildings burned down in another forest fire leaving behind only a barn. This still stands on the north side of Vine Hill Road in a grove of redwood trees.

Guests of Glenwood Magnetic Springs posing for the camera on the meadow beside the main hotel building, circa 1890. (*UC Santa Cruz*)

Guests relaxing outside two large cottages at Glenwood Magnetic Springs, circa 1890. Photo by W. A. Bell. (*Author's collection*)

A view of Summer Home Farm and the Bean Creek basin from above the vineyard, 1923. (*UC Santa Cruz*)

A man reading in a redwood grove on the grounds of Summer Home Farm, circa 1900. (*Author's collection*)

Summer Home Farm (1875 – 1915)

John Wesley DeWolf bought 298.75 acres on the eastern bank of Bean Creek three miles south of Glenwood around 1868. In May 1875, he and his father Benjamin R. DeWolfe opened DeWolfe's Magnetic Springs, at the same time naming the property Strawberry Valley after the wild (though well-tended) strawberries that grew there. John had lived in the Scotts Valley area since at least 1871 and was active in the school district and general life of the community. He grew wine grapes, planted fruit trees, and raised hay and grains, but he also maintained areas of wildflowers and woodland for visitors to the property. His magnetic springs, like its better-known rival, focused primarily on treating the infirm via water with magnetic properties. The family only ran the resort for a year or so, and eventually sold the property in 1882 to Brainard C. Brown.

Brown initially retained the name Strawberry Valley for the area, but he soon settled upon the name Summer Home Farm to market his resort. By 1883, he had added a commodious hotel, cozy cottages, and a large campground to the property. Brown also seasonally dammed Bean Creek to create an artificial swimming, boating, and fishing lake. Horseback riding on rented horses and coach rides to the Santa Cruz beach were the most heavily-emphasized offerings of the resort in newspaper advertisements. Summer Home Farm remained a functioning farm throughout its time as a vacation destination. Brown planted new crops annually, including orchard fruits and grape vines, while maintaining a healthy herd of Jersey cattle. He even experimented with fruit drying in the late 1880s.

In early 1892, J. Bernheim & Company acquired Summer Home Farm in a sheriff's auction. Why Brown lost the property in the first place is unclear. The company appears to have consisted entirely of members of the Bernheim family, several of whom had visited the resort repeatedly in 1891. The first year that they owned it, the Bernheims planted over 4,600 fruit trees on the estate, mostly prunes and pears. They hired Domingo Oliver to oversee the orchards and vineyard, and Chinese workers to pick and pack the fruits. Other than relatives and family friends, few people vacationed at Summer Home Farm in the first five years that the Bernheims owned it.

In January 1897, the Bernheims hired Capt. Julius H. and Frank Haesters to look after the resort side of Summer Home Farm. The resort did well during these years, with Frank Haesters managing day-to-day operations and the Bernheims remaining in charge of the working farm. Hundreds of people flocked to the farm on weekends, while dozens remained throughout the summer months. The Haesters were leading champions of establishing a formal station at Clems, but the best they could manage was having a shelter erected. This was useful for guests familiar with the area, but new visitors still arrived at Glenwood Station.

The new century heralded a change in ownership of Summer Home Farm. The Bernheims sold the property to Wilbur B. Hugus and brothers Harrison "Harry" W. and Mulford Haines for $9,500 on December 18, 1900. Two years later, in April 1902, Hugus sold his interest to the Haines. Meanwhile, Capt. Haesters stayed on as proprietor of the resort and continued to expand the amenities there. He added a dining room, six new cottages, and twelve guest rooms to the main hotel. However, the Haines would have to run the property themselves since Haesters quit in October 1901 to manage Villa Fontenay. After a problematic 1902 season, the Haines shut the resort down before the 1903 season to make improvements. Nothing in the newspapers suggests they actually made any changes, though, and only a small number of visitors came in 1904 and 1905.

Clearly the Haines had tired of the resort and they searched for interested buyers. In July 1905, they sold the property for $15,000 to Now Folk, a New Thought organization based out of San Francisco that was seeking a mountain resort. The group was "neither a religious or a social reform organization. It is a small body of people who believe simply in making the best of life.... our idea is to be happy now, wherever we are, to be healthful now and to do all the good we can right here and now." They turned the resort into a health center and summer school for members and visitors alike and appointed their secretary, Sam Exton Foulds, as its first manager. When the San Francisco Earthquake struck, the resort continued operating without a break, with Foulds even remarking to the *Santa Cruz Sentinel* that he expected a better year with so many people in San Francisco seeking an escape.

By 1909, "Now" Mt. Home, as it was renamed, had become the base for the Now Folk. The organization was formally incorporated on December 22, 1911, with the Chappell family the most prominent shareholders and the leaders of the movement. However, the resort declined throughout the 1910s. All advertisements disappeared from newspapers and all discussion of it dropped. It is possible that the Now Folk ran out on their mortgage for the property around 1913 and it fell back into the hands of the Haines brothers. Whoever owned it around 1915 sold 207 acres of the property to George and Ida Reid, who ran the property as a private home and ranch for around thirty years.

One of the reasons for the resort's decline was certainly the arrival of the automobile. Immediately before and after World War I, Bean Creek Road was graded through to Scotts Valley while construction shut down the Glenwood to Scotts Valley section of what would become the Glenwood Highway. This greatly increased automobile traffic in the area, disturbing the peace and serenity the resort had long marketed as perks. When the road was completed, the Reids remodeled and then reopened Summer Home Farm, though no advertisements from this time have survived. They rented hotel rooms and several cabins, and the resort featured a pool, tennis courts, and various indoor and outdoor recreational facilities. A son, Roy Reid, also ran a small sawmill on the property during the 1930s. The Great Depression combined with the Reids' old age led them to close the resort following the 1937 summer season.

During World War II, the resort may have been leased to the YWCA for use as a women's summer camp. In 1945, it was sold for $30,000 to the Salvation Army, which planned to convert the property into one of its core West Coast boys' summer camps. When it finally opened on July 4, 1946, the Salvation Army rechristened the property Camp Redwood Glen, which remains an active camp and conference center today.

Boys looking at something in the former vineyards of Summer Home Farm at Camp Redwood Glen, late 1940s. The former farmhouse and several guest cabins can be seen in the background. (*Santa Cruz Public Libraries*)

Glenwood Hotel (1883 – 1924)

It should come as no surprise that Charles C. Martin, the unofficial mayor and leader of the Glenwood community, ran perhaps the most successful resort along Bean Creek. Yet his path to opening the hotel was not straight. He ran the Felton Livery Stable with partners for several years in the late 1860s and early 1870s. In 1875, he became joint owner of the Santa Cruz House. Throughout this time, he also owned his property in Glenwood and remained active in the community, especially in having a road graded from Mountain Charlie's toll road to his property and ensuring that the South Pacific Coast Railroad passed through the Bean Creek basin. This latter feat proved important to the history of his hotel.

Around September 1880, Martin left his role managing the Santa Cruz House and settled in Glenwood permanently. While he helped establish the community's first post office, school, and store, he took his time in building a resort on his property. His land did not have the rustic appeal of Summer Home Farm nor the medicinal benefits of Glenwood Magnetic Springs, but he had his long experience as a hotelier. In 1883, he erected a hotel of unknown design capable of accommodating at least seventy-five guests. However, nothing is said of it again and it is unclear if it ever hosted guests. In April 1886, Martin opened Glenwood Park on his property beside the railroad tracks. This was a large picnic area that had a mid-sized outdoor dancing pavilion. Martin made certain to emphasize the

Multi-panel postcard showcasing features of Glenwood Hotel, including wagon rides, an automobile, and rustic cottages, circa 1910. (*Sourisseau Academy*)

The dance and dining halls at Glenwood Hotel, circa 1900. (*Jay Topping*)

A cottage beside the forest at Glenwood Hotel, circa 1910. (*Gil Pennington*)

picnic ground's proximity to the railroad depot, and the venue did well for several years, attracting thousands of visitors annually.

Ultimately, Charles Martin does not appear to be the one who opened a popular hotel on his Glenwood property. That honor went to his son, William H. Martin, who first began entertaining guests when he took over the estate in 1894. His hotel had no formal name until spring 1897, when the first advertisement for the Glenwood Hotel appeared in the *San Francisco Examiner*. The resort was situated above Parker Creek, a tributary stream of Bean Creek, and beside the Martin family's hay fields. It benefited from a large grove of old-growth redwood trees that Charles had refused to cut down.

The core building of the resort was the hotel structure, a two-story building situated immediately beside the old Martin family home. Over its twelve years in operation, Martin added many cottages, a campground, a cement swimming pool fed by Bean Creek, a baseball diamond, a men's saloon and smoking parlor beneath an outdoor dance floor, and a small woodland theatre for community productions. For meals, he provided milk from the family's cows, and vegetables and fruits from their gardens and orchards.

As with the proprietors of some of the other nearby resorts, William hoped to benefit from the disastrous 1906 San Francisco Earthquake by attracting people to the mountains as an escape. Just days after the catastrophe, he bought advertisements in several regional papers inviting people to his hotel. Whether this actually worked is unclear, since the journey was difficult thanks to the closure of the railroad route between Glenwood and the Bay Area. However, William became creative and built his own twelve-seater automobile, which began shuttling people between the Santa Cruz depot and Glenwood only six weeks after the temblor.

The reopening of the railroad line in spring 1909 prompted a renewed interest in the Glenwood area and its resorts. William added several new cottages to the Glenwood Hotel, while Charles seems to have added some cottages to nearby Glenwood Park. Throughout 1910, the Glenwood Hotel averaged 115 guests, prompting William to plan an addition to the main hotel building, though this was probably never built. Visitor numbers plummeted as the 1910s progressed, and around the time of the United States' entry into World War I, William closed down the hotel.

In January 1920, Percy D. Lowell leased half of the Martin family's property, including the Glenwood Hotel. Lowell hoped that the Glenwood Highway, which was completed before the start of the summer season, would bring a new generation of vacationers to Glenwood. In preparation for their arrival,

Glenwood Hotel viewed from the road, circa 1920. (*Sourisseau Academy*)

William Martin at the wheel of his custom automobile with a car full of women and children, circa 1908. (*California State Library*)

he made several improvements, including the addition of electrical lighting and the repainting of a cottage in pink to function as a honeymoon suite. The visitors came, but they mostly passed through. In 1921, William sued Lowell for denying him access to his property to harvest his crops. William won the case in February 1922 and took back control of the property, but he chose not to reopen the hotel.

In 1935, at the height of the Great Depression, the hotel and Glenwood Park were repurposed as a camp for State Emergency Relief Administration (SERA) workers, who came to the area to upgrade bridges, roads, and other infrastructure. In March 1936, a Dominican group, Sisters of St. Mary's of the Palms, based out of Mission San José in Frémont, leased the former resort from William Martin's widow, Emma, for use as a summer boarding and day school. The camp opened the following year and the group purchased the property outright in 1938. The main hotel, several cottages, and the Martin family's home were demolished in 1970. The site is now a sprawling meadow.

A view of Glenwood Hotel from high above Bean Creek showing the entry road, meadows, and orchards, circa 1910. (*Santa Cruz Museum of Art & History*)

Close-up view of Glenwood Hotel, probably shortly after it closed, circa 1925. (*Author's collection*)

People playing a game of baseball on the diamond beside the Glenwood Hotel, circa 1910. (*Author's collection*)

FOOT BRIDGE - GLENWOOD, CAL.

Two men posing for the camera on a footbridge over Parker Creek near Glenwood Hotel, circa 1920. (*Author's collection*)

Pathway to Glenwood Hotel along the forest edge, circa 1910. (*UC Santa Cruz*)

Glenwood Hotel shortly before it was demolished, 1960s. (*Jay Topping*)

Mount Pleasant Farm (1886 – 1919)

Situated next door to Summer Home Farm above Bean Creek, Mount Pleasant Farm was established in 1886 by William B. and Christina Knox. Compared to the other hotels in the area, this small resort located four miles south of Glenwood has very little known about it. No photographs or advertisements seem to exist, suggesting it was not marketed locally. The Knox family moved to Santa Cruz in 1919 and sold their property to George Perkut, Angelo Vuinovich, and Joe Iskra.

Now going under the name Mt. Pleasant Ranch, Perkut and Vuinovich (Iskra left shortly after acquiring the property) primarily logged the property to make railroad ties between 1920 and 1921. However, there is at least limited evidence that they leased some of the resort's cabins to vacationers. A fire in August 1921, however, ended their plans when it burned through the cottage city and their yard of unshipped timber products. In 1923, Edward J. McCarthy took over, but by this point it operated as an occasional resort, mostly for associates of McCarthy. The resort is last mentioned in newspapers in 1941, when William Knox passed away. Christina had died in 1932 after an illness of over twenty years.

Vacationers fishing on Bean Creek near Glenwood, circa 1890. (*Edward Fenn*)

Gibbs' Resort (1900 – 1916)

Gibbs' Resort was the last substantial resort in the Santa Cruz Mountains that catered exclusively to railroad traffic. San Francisco restauranteur Albert W. J. Gibbs retired to the 200-acre property around 1899 after fighting years of illness in the city. By 1900, he began making plans for his resort. His property sat on the ridgeline that separated the Bean Creek and Zayante Creek watersheds. As such, travelers coming from the Bay Area would arrive at the resort via Glenwood Station, while travelers from the south used Zayante Station. Unlike other resorts in the Glenwood area, Gibbs' Resort was in an area of chaparral, with sand hills and pine trees replacing mountain streams and redwoods. This made it a unique destination.

A post office was established on the property on November 28, 1900, which likely marked the beginning of its life as a resort. Gibbs incorporated the Gibbs' Co-operative Colony around the same time to finance the construction of the resort, which he estimated would cost $50,000. He hoped this would cover the cost of upgrading the property's existing infrastructure and the cost of new buildings, such as cabins, a cookhouse, and support structures. Once its task was done, the company was dissolved and the De La Roza Profit Sharing Association arose in its place. Named after Gibbs' wife's maiden name, this new firm was responsible for managing the property long term. The company subdi-

Gibbs Ranch southwest of Glenwood atop the Zayante-Bean Creek divide, circa 1911. (*Richard Holland*)

vided the property into 36 lots and set up a grocery store, hotel, and restaurant, as well as a working farm to raise poultry and grow fruits and vegetables. Gibbs also hoped to grow wine grapes. Thus, he planned to create a small town as much as a resort, seeking both seasonal visitors and potential year-round residents. Although most newspapers simply called the property Gibbs' Resort, it was marketed as De La Rosa Resort from 1905.

According to his own reports, Gibbs attracted hundreds of visitors to his resort over its first two years of operation. Gibbs built a switch-backing road down from the resort to Zayante Station and picked up customers in his personal coach. Indeed, he had an entire network of narrow roads built atop the ridge. The San Francisco Earthquake, though, seems to have slowed down traffic, as very little is said of the resort in newspapers after 1906. In 1909, with the reopening of the railroad through the mountains, Gibbs' Resort began its second life. In 1910, it was rebranded Gibbs' Scenic Resort, with its campgrounds, croquet grounds, restaurant, and views of the Monterey Bay emphasized in its advertising. Then, in 1911, the resort was renamed again to Gibbs' Ranch, with a tagline: "Not a Hotel." By this point, everyday management had passed to George L. Claussenius. E. M. Gallup took over in 1913, simplifying the property's name to Gibbs Resort. This was the name that stuck for the remainder of its existence. G. W. Paulsen became the resort's last manager in 1914.

What precisely happened to the resort over the subsequent years is unclear, but the post office shifted to Zayante Station on January 29, 1916. Gibbs' wife died in 1919 and left her family's estate in Boulder Creek to her husband, who moved there in 1920. In 1922, Gibbs opened the New Alpine Hotel on Central Avenue in Boulder Creek. At the same time, he leased his Glenwood property to A. H. Buckley of San Francisco, who intended to use it as a private chicken farm. Gibbs was still involved in the property, though, as he made several improvements to the cottages and outbuildings that same year. What happened next to the former Gibbs' Resort is unknown, but Gibbs lost most of his money during the first few years of the Great Depression. He died at the age of 75 on April 27, 1932. Around 1971, the former resort was subdivided into the Weston Road housing development. The Gibbs' old road to Zayante Station still exists as a poorly-maintained exit road in case of emergency, while the resort's old cookhouse is now a private residence that goes by the name Gibbs Station.

Advertisement in the Pacific Coast Gazette listing properties for sale from the de la Roza Profit Sharing Association at Gibbs Resort, January 1908.

View of Lovers' Lane at Gibbs Resort, circa 1907. (*Ronnie Trubek*)

Gibbs Station sign over the driveway to Gibbs Resort's former cookhouse, now a private residence on Weston Road. Photo by Derek R. Whaley. (*Author's collection*)

Villa Fontenay (1901 – 1930)

Located off Vine Hill Road near the Magnetic Springs, Villa Fontenay did not begin its life as a resort. The property was originally owned by John W. Jarvis, a local vintner who was seeking profitable locations to grow grapes. He had settled there in the 1860s and established, among other things, the community's school on a corner of the property. Around 1876, Governor Washington Bartlett acquired the property in a mortgage sale and soon entrusted it to his daughter, Nellie. Nellie and her husband, French immigrant Henry Mel de Fontenay, ran a vineyard on the 250-acre property from 1879. When Bartlett died on September 12, 1887, he bequeathed the property to his wife, Clara N. Mann, who died June 8, 1890, at which point Nellie inherited it.

The Mels ran the Villa Fontenay winery throughout their two decades of ownership. In fact, they were responsible for introducing the first vines of sauvignon blanc, sauvignon vert, and muscadelle de bordelaise to California. They won awards for their wines in 1884 and Henri became Santa Cruz County's wine inspector. By 1893, the vintners of Vine Hill were producing 100,000 gallons of wine per year, as well as thousands of boxes of grapes. Meanwhile, the Mels' Vine Hill home, Villa Fontenay, was completed in November 1888.

Unfortunately, the family went bankrupt in 1900 and the property was foreclosed. Frederick W. Billing bought it from the bank and hired Capt. J. W. Haesters to help turn it into a destination resort. They enlarged the house and

View of Villa Fontenay from the top of Vine Hill, 1880. (*Author's collection*)

turned it into a 14-room hotel, which featured a panoramic view of the entire Soquel Creek basin, with the Monterey Bay and Pacific Ocean visible in the distance. They also added several large, eight-room cottages, which dotted the surrounding hillside. The initial complex included croquet and tennis courts, a bowling alley, and an amusement hall for billiards. Electric lights were installed across the facility for night-time events. More cottages were added in 1902, and the dining room and kitchen were enlarged to commercial standards. They also extended lighting along many of the surrounding paths. Before their third season, Billings and Haesters added enough extra rooms to support fifty more guests, increasing the capacity of the resort to 150 vacationers. At the same time, they added a second bowling lane to the alley. In 1904, following the death of Haester's wife, J. E. Moore took over management of the resort.

In February 1905, Billing sold Villa Fontenay to John A. Nordin, who hired Rice Harper as his new proprietor. Harper oversaw the addition of two large hotel annexes near the original Mel home. The resort remained popular for another ten years, advertised in newspapers almost daily for much of this time. When the United States entered World War I, Billings stopped advertising the resort, trusting word of mouth to sell rooms during the summer months. According to local legend, the hotel may have run a speakeasy during Prohibition.

Villa Fontenay survived the advent of the automobile only to be shut down due to the Great Depression. At some point in the 1930s, Dr. Alexander Thomas Leonard purchased the property and used it as a private home. In 1958, it was purchased by the United Airlines' Mainliner Club for use as a recreation facility for members, but the company abandoned its plans soon after. In 1962, Cave Realty purchased the property and planned to convert it into a trailer park. This idea met difficulties when it was determined that the water system would need expensive upgrades and that a formal highway interchange would be required on Highway 17.

The Mel family had long sought to reclaim their lost ancestral home and, in 1972, a granddaughter of Henri and Nellie Mel, Dorothy Mel Kulp, managed to buy the property. Three years later, two large fires destroyed most of the estate, with only the main house and the former schoolhouse left standing. Dorothy decided to cut and sell the remaining standing timber and subdivide the property. Today, the Villa Fontenay area still goes by its historic name and is used for wine-making, although there is no longer a resort of any manner there. Most of the region is populated by mansions with manicured lawns and swimming pools, thereby retaining its status as a beautiful haven within the mountains.

Vacationers relaxing on the deck of a cottage at Villa Fontenay, circa 1905. (*Gil Pennington*)

Revelers in a gazebo beside the main hotel building of Villa Fontenay, circa 1905. (*Gil Pennington*)

Four bowlers chatting at the bowling alley at Villa Fontenay, circa 1905. (*Gil Pennington*)

Two men playing billiards in the poolhall at Villa Fontenay, circa 1905. (*Gil Pennington*)

Vineyard and residence of Henry Mel on Vine Hill, circa 1880. Photo by Carleton E. Watkins. (*California State Library*)

Stereograph of Vine Hill looking southeast along the Coast Range, circa 1880. Photo by Carleton E. Watkins. (*California State Library*)

Four-frame panorama of Villa Fontenay looking south down Branciforte Creek, circa 1900. (*Gil Pennington*)

EASTWARD							SAN FRANCISCO SUBDIVISION		WESTWARD				
	FIRST CLASS						Time Table No. 147 March 30, 1940 San Jose-Santa Cruz Branch		**FIRST CLASS**				
Capacity of sidings and spurs in car lengths	138	32	168	34	46		STATIONS		123	31	185	45	33
	Passenger	Santa Cruz	Passenger	Passenger	Passenger				Passenger	Santa Cruz	Passenger	Passenger	Passenger
		5.18 PM		9.45 AM	5.55 AM	46.9	SAN JOSE	23.6	s 8.34 AM	s 3.21 PM	7.27 PM		s 8.37 PM
						47.6	W. P. R. R. Crossing	23.1					
				f 9.53	6.07	60.7	CAMPBELL	18.0	f	3.09	7.15		f 8.29
	6.37 PM	5.28	2.30 PM	f 9.58	6.15	62.3	VASONA JUNCTION	27.4	s 6.55 AM	8.24	3.00	7.06	f 8.24
	s 6.46 PM	5.36	2.40 PM	s 10.06	s 6.25 AM	54.5	LOS GATOS	24.5	6.49 AM	8.18	2.50 PM	6.56 PM	s 8.18
		f 5.45		f 10.15		57.0	ALMA	22.2		f 8.07			f 8.07
		f 5.58		f 10.28		61.5	WRIGHT	17.5		f 7.54			f 7.55
		f		f		63.4	LAUREL	15.3		f			f
		f 6.13		f 10.43		64.8	GLENWOOD	14.4		f 7.39			f 7.41
		f		f		65.5	TANK SIDING	13.6		f			f
		f 6.23		f 10.53		68.5	MEEHAN	10.5		f 7.29			f 7.31
		f 6.27		f 10.57		70.4	OLYMPIA	8.5		f 7.25			f 7.27
		f		f		72.1	MT. HERMON	7.1		f			f
		s 6.34		s 11.04		70.4	FELTON	6.5		s 7.18			s 7.21
		f		f		73.3	BIG TREES	6.9		f			f
		f 6.42		f 11.12		75.4	RINCON	3.5		f			f 7.10
		f		f		76.0	EBLIS	1.5		f			f
		s 6.53 PM		s 11.26 AM		76.5	SANTA CRUZ	0.0	7.00 AM				7.00 PM

Southern Pacific, Coast Division employee timetable no. 147, showing the final schedule for the route through the Santa Cruz Mountains, March 30, 1940. Clems was still listed as a flag-stop for passing trains. (*Author's Collection*)

The U.S. Army First Infantry raising the Stars and Stripes over Glenwood School, September 18, 1896. The unit was marching from "Camp Garfield" (Garfield Park in Santa Cruz) to Angel Island, San Francisco. (*UC Santa Cruz*)

SELECT
BIBLIOGRAPHY

Clark, Donald T. *Santa Cruz County Place Names: A Geographical Dictionary*. 2nd edition. Santa Cruz, CA: Museum of Art & History, 2002.

Dunn, Geoffrey. "The Ghosts of Glenwood: The Little Town of Glenwood and Its Nearby Magnetic Springs were Once Major Tourist Attractions." *Santa Cruz Style* 24 (2013), 60-63.

Gibson, Ross Eric. "A History of Wine Making in the Santa Cruz Mountains." Santa Cruz Public Libraries—Local History. https://history.santacruzpl.org/omeka/items/show/134398. Accessed February 19, 2023.

Hamman, Rick. *California Central Coast Railways*. 2nd edition. Santa Cruz, CA: Otter B Books, 2002.

Harrison, Edward S. *History of Santa Cruz County California*. San Francisco, CA: Pacific Press Publishing, 1892.

Koch, Margaret. "Glenwood: Charlie Martin's Town." *Santa Cruz County History Journal 1* (1994), 107-111.

Koch, Margaret. *Santa Cruz County: Parade of the Past*. Santa Cruz, CA: Western Tanager Press/Valley Publishers, 1973.

Logan, Clarence A. "Limestone in California." *California Journal of Mines and Geology* 43:3 (July 1947), 175-357.

MacGregor, Bruce A., and Richard Truesdale. *South Pacific Coast: A Centennial*. Boulder, CO: Pruett Publishing, 1982.

Payne, Stephen Michael. "A Howling Wilderness: Resorts in the Summit Road Area." Santa Cruz Public Libraries—Local History. https://history.santacruzpl.org/omeka/items/show/134527. Accessed February 19, 2023.

Powell, Ronald G. *The Reign of the Lumber Barons: Part Two of the History of Rancho Soquel Augmentation*. Edited by Derek R. Whaley. Santa Cruz, CA: Zayante Publishing, 2021.

—. *The Shadow of Loma Prieta: Part Three of the History of Rancho Soquel Augmentation*. Edited by Derek R. Whaley. Santa Cruz, CA: Zayante Publishing, 2022.

—. *The Tragedy of Martina Castro: Part One of the History of Rancho Soquel Augmentation*. Edited by Derek R. Whaley. Santa Cruz, CA: Zayante Publishing, 2020.

Whaley, Derek R. *Santa Cruz Trains: Railroads of the Santa Cruz Mountains*. Santa Cruz, CA, 2015.

Young, John V. *Ghost Towns of the Santa Cruz Mountains*. 3rd edition. Lafayette, CA: Great West Books, 2002.

For a complete history of the railroad that once ran between Los Gatos and Santa Cruz, as well as its branch lines to Felton, Boulder Creek, and beyond, check out . . .

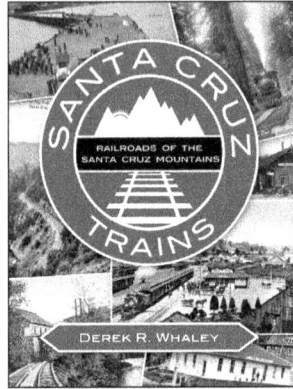

Santa Cruz Trains:
Railroads of the
Santa Cruz Mountains
by Derek R. Whaley

Be sure to check out these other titles available now from Zayante Publishing:

Santa Cruz Trains: Reflections on the Mountain Route
by Derek R. Whaley

The Secret History of Santa Cruz County series
The Tragedy of Martina: Part One of the
History of Rancho Soquel Augmentation
by Ronald G. Powell, edited by Derek R. Whaley

The Reign of the Lumber Barons: Part Two of the
History of Rancho Soquel Augmentation
by Ronald G. Powell, edited by Derek R. Whaley

The Shadow of Loma Prieta: Part Three of the
History of Rancho Soquel Augmentation
by Ronald G. Powell, edited by Derek R. Whaley

www.ingramcontent.com/pod-product-compliance
Lightning Source LLC
Chambersburg PA
CBHW060403090426
42734CB00011B/2241